A Given Life

A Given Life

The Encouragement of Grace

Jean McAllister

RESOURCE *Publications* · Eugene, Oregon

A GIVEN LIFE
The Encouragement of Grace

Resource Publications
An Imprint of Wipf and Stock Publishers
199 W. 8th Ave., Suite 3
Eugene, OR 97401

www.wipfandstock.com

PAPERBACK ISBN: 978-1-5326-0982-4
HARDCOVER ISBN: 978-1-5326-0984-8
EBOOK ISBN: 978-1-5326-0983-1

Manufactured in the U.S.A.   FEBRUARY 17, 2017

To my daughters: Cathleen Crosby, Xan Blackburn, P. J. Vinke

"We live the given life, and not the planned."[1]

Yes, what you send, Lord, is what I live,
not planned, nor could be, since it flows
from your hand, your forgiving heart,
which now demands all I have to give.

Your command is now, for me unplanned,
my good, and my delight; in joy I go
along the pleasant boundary lines
that you have set to bless, protect and show

your love to me specific, known
in your past-finding-out ways;
your ways are high ways, now becoming mine,
the given life which will in grace be crowned.

1. Berry, *This Day*, 150.

Contents

Preface

"You should write a book," they told me. Over the course of my ten years in Rwanda, I heard this suggestion often. But I never felt I "should" write a book; in fact, I was pretty sure I should not. There were already too many books. I didn't want to add to their number, unless I felt there was a compelling reason.

Some years along, as the encouragement to write continued coming, a conjunction of pointed email messages and a movement in my spirit directed me to the admission that indeed, I "should" write a book. I came to believe this was God's nudging, his idea.

From the beginning, I have prayed and hoped this work would be encouraging to any who read it. I have learned through my failures and victories that the God I believe in is a God of encouragement. I often think Paul's self-characterization as "the chief of sinners" applies to me. But God has made a way for me, and for everyone, to taste the goodness of his steadfast love through the knowledge of Jesus Christ. I have written my testimony here—how God sent his word out again and again until I could hear it, believe it, and live by it. His word never returns to him without accomplishing the purpose he had in mind for it. He has given me a life far different than I could have planned or imagined, and every phase and piece of it has been for the purpose of drawing me closer to himself, so that I could show people all that he has done for me. I want to give God all the glory.

In telling my story, in particular the part in Rwanda, I also relate some of the difficulties I encountered in this little country in the very heart of Africa. I was a missionary there, serving on my own, but under the umbrella of a local nongovernmental organization. Along the way, I often became not only frustrated, but angry, because of certain troubling aspects of the Rwandan culture and character. I was thrust into a challenge to love and serve people, some of whom were impossible, in human terms, to love. But I have been told by others familiar with Rwanda that writing about my experience would encourage others going through similar cross-cultural exigencies, and perhaps help prepare others who are considering doing such work. I hope that may be so, but the primary focus throughout is to show God's persistent encouragement, not only in Rwanda—which after all comprises only ten years—but from the difficult beginnings of my life to the present, a span of eighty years. My times are in God's hands, and it may be that I will be in his presence soon. I hope he will be pleased with this effort to show his majesty, love, and sustaining grace.

They say that no experience is wasted. The Apostle Paul affirms that for those who love God and are called according to his purpose, he works all things for good—somehow (see Rom 8:28). How we understand "good" makes a difference in our interpretation of this familiar verse. My take is that I must accept this on faith. I may never perceive or understand the good God will bring about. I trust that these pages may show God's redemption power in one life, mine, in taking a terribly broken and wrong-hearted person in hand. I hope they show a mighty and merciful God who seems intent on transforming and using such a person, wasting nothing of the past.

This memoir is arranged as a collection of poems, journal entries, and narratives, all gathering up in diverse ways to form reflections upon the encouragement of grace. Although my witness arises from my wretched personal story, the key thing is that God is glorified in that story because of what he made of it, and what he made of me. That is the story I "should" tell, and I have tried my best to trace that journey in these pages.

Acknowledgments

I WANT TO THANK all those friends who kept insisting I should write a book such as this. I am most grateful to my early readers, who gave me reason to believe I should persevere: Margie Gilchrist, Billie Ylvisaker, and Sally Stuart. Additional thanks go to my friend Billie Ylvisaker, who also spent hours attending to every detail in formatting the text. Thanks also to my editor, Matthew Wimer of Wipf and Stock, who kept me on track with the project. I am especially grateful for the loving support of my three daughters, to whom this book is dedicated, and finally, for the presence and encouragement of the Holy Spirit of God who sustained and guided me throughout.

1

Memory and Faith

THIS BOOK IS AN attempt to reflect on some parts of my journey as a follower of Jesus Christ. It is, as Gilbert and Sullivan say, "a thing of shreds and patches," but it has a consistent pattern, if only known to the God who created me.

From the moment I arrived in Rwanda, aged sixty-eight, people called me *umukecuru*, a term of respect used for women old enough to know something of the way of the world. It can mean either "old woman" or, most often, "mother." This designation was for me both warming and humbling. I was not a good mother, nor did I have my own mother to nurture me growing up. Further, I had a neurotic, brilliant, and damaging stepmother whom I both loved and feared. Now in Rwanda I was being called "mother." This theme of "mother" threads from my birth through my own failure as a mother to this new land in which no one knew what sort of person I was. People simply took me for a wise woman, a nurturer, a mother. This perspective colored and shaped my years in Rwanda.

Concerning my time in Rwanda, a few things have come clear: First, I knew I was called to live in Rwanda; second, it was hard; third, God sustained me; and last, God used me. This is not only a book about a relatively short period of my life, the Rwanda years; it is also about redemption, transformation, and renewal. I am a witness to God's grace, kindness, patience, and mercy, poured out to me and to everyone who believes in an unrestrained stream. It is that which I hope will shine through. My self is only of value as it is renewed after the image of its Creator, and that is a lifelong process, a journey. As they say in Rwanda, "I'm on my way coming."

As I begin, I am confronted with a problem: my memory is "fallen," along with the rest of me; it functions poorly, inconsistently, and usually unfaithfully. I find this out, of course, after the fact—long afterwards, in most cases. Someone sheds light on a piece of my past, and I suddenly see that I had it all wrong, that I had an incomplete framework or perspective. This phenomenon continues; even within a ten-year span, such as forms the major part of this book, I learn how unreliable my memory is. Reviewing and musing on the journals I have kept, I discover not only incidents I had forgotten, but patterns and insights that recur—many discovered as if for the first time.

When I think of my childhood, I "remember" certain things which have later been shown to be incorrect, or imperfectly remembered. I suppose I'm not alone in this respect. For example, I had thought for years after leaving home that my family was poor. It was a "memory" based on the extreme anxiety of my stepmother about finances, but I didn't know that until years later. One day I happened to be considering the benefits I enjoyed growing up. These included lessons—piano, ballet, and voice—summer camp for eight weeks each year in the Adirondacks, and private girls' school. I lived in a house on fourteen acres of meadows, gardens, and orchards—graced by two-hundred-year-old maples and other grand trees for climbing; a house with so many rooms I had to count them up in my mind (small rooms, but still . . .). It dawned on me then that my memory of being poor couldn't be correct. It was an unsettling new awareness, shifting something within me to make adjustments. The truth was that I grew up in a well-to-do home, but with a mentality of being poor. This created an awkward inner tension, the effects of which no doubt have been working their way through my life orientation ever since.

Again, just recently, I realized something else about my childhood home. This wasn't exactly a memory correction, but rather, a pleasant revelation springing from a new awareness. I was reading a book called *Gods at War* by Kyle Idleman, in which he writes about how all of us can get caught up in "worshiping" something other than God (as revealed in the Bible, and especially in Jesus Christ). As he invited his readers to consider "old gods"—those we may have mindlessly carried with us into adult life—I looked again at my childhood home, to see what my parents (who were not Christians) believed in, or "worshiped." I was struck by God's grace in setting me in such a home. My parents valued things I consider to be good: intellect, books, nature, all kinds of creativity, and peace in the world.

My dad was passionate about trying to get the government to change its military priorities, which he felt resulted in depriving people all around the world of basic necessities. My folks valued doing things the right way (not slipshod or inefficiently), speaking the truth, and working hard. They also valued a world perspective. My dad did a major development project (business-oriented) in Liberia, in connection with the Liberia Company, a United States government venture started in 1948 by Secretary of State Edward Stettinius. Every Thanksgiving we would have guests from some foreign place at our table.

My dad was a man of integrity, I always felt. He tried to understand what was the right thing to do and then to do it. These are all terrific values to be immersed in growing up. There were difficulties in relationships with my parents—both between them and between them and me—but the setting, the ambiance, and the rich matrix of benefits were a gracious mitigation of the difficulties I experienced.

The "gods" my parents worshiped were limited in their effectiveness, but I believe my parents were true to them, and they could have been stepping stones to a deeper and more complete understanding of reality for them. As far as I know, they never came to see the truth as it is in Jesus before they died. I see those "gods" as a kind of tutor in my childhood—much as Paul views the law's purpose for the Jews (see Gal 3:24). One can serve and try to live up to its requirements—and discover one's immeasurable limitations—but ultimately there is an all-encompassing God, who is the source of all these good things and who extends far beyond all of them.

So how can I write about my life in any true sense if this is the case with my fallen, faulty, misguided memory? It must be a work of faith. I must enter into the task with humility, knowing at the start that I may not always get it right—even about myself, which I should know more about than anything else.

I often read Psalm 139, and I love the flow of David's ideas, starting with his awareness of God's searching spirit, which has probed so deeply into David's inner being, causing him to cry, "Such knowledge is too wonderful for me; it is so high that I cannot attain it" (Ps 139:6). God is the one who knows me, having made me, putting his infinite mind to my very molecules so as to arrange them in a particular and unique way. There is no possibility of fathoming God's knowledge of me. But, as David does at the end, I can invite this God who knows me to search me—so that I may know something of what God knows of me.

And this is what I do. I invite God to look into my heart, to see if there is some hurtful way that needs to be brought to the light and dealt with by his consuming love. I believe I can trust God to do this searching and exposing, right to the end of my life. And this is the basis on which I can establish my writing: I report what I learn along the way—knowing it is incomplete in many ways—and trust God to weave this reporting together so that others may be encouraged to let God search them, and reveal them to themselves. In the process—the real encouragement—we find out who God is. In revealing us to ourselves, he reveals himself. Seeing ourselves as God sees us necessarily reveals God's values and holy standards, as well as his steadfast love.

Moses wanted to see God. He, more than perhaps anyone else in the Bible, knew God—he had countless encounters with God, who treated Moses as a friend, sharing all his great plans with him. But Moses still longed to see God (see Exod 33). He needed to know that God's presence would always go with him. That longing is planted in me. I believe it is deep in every person. No matter how long I've known God and have had amazing, intimate, and surprising interactions with God, I still long to know him. He is *beyond* my human knowledge, so such longing will always be appropriate.

This writing is about God-in-me, and me-in-God. I hope to show who I am and am becoming as God works and moves in me, speaks to me, and empowers me. Anyone can do this. Everyone has a me-in-God story, if they have begun to walk with God. And each story is unique and valuable, worth sharing with others. This is my attempt, and my prayer is to be authentic, to encourage others with the encouragement God has given me, and to glorify his name.

2

Intimations

I IMAGINE THAT WHEN I am face-to-face with Jesus in the new Earth and new Heaven, I will be able to look back over the ways he had led me, from the earliest days of my life, until the day I found out who he truly was and wanted to have him at the center of my life. I can find out hints of his ways through reflection, and more and more are revealed, the longer I live. There has been a gradual pulling aside of a curtain, letting me see some of the simple, ordinary events of my life as preparation for his coming into my heart for good.

C. S. Lewis wrote his story of being "surprised by joy"—coming to faith through the pathway of delight in beauty, literature, and creation. I recently was considering the question of what, and how, I love, because what one loves or takes joy in can be what God will use to bring a person to faith in him as the giver of all delights.

Here are some of the things I love:

- snow-covered mountains against blue sky

- new buds on trees

- warm sun, for basking

- lying down after a full and tiring day

- Christian fellowship, and experiencing the movements of the Holy Spirit

- children's voices at play; a comfortable and familiar cat

- flowers
- Adirondack lakes, canoeing; Lake Kivu—mysterious, vast, silent
- faces of friends
- colors, birdsong, woods
- my children, grandchildren, and great-grandchildren; and that they love each other
- the Kinyarwanda language
- singing; dancing
- music—classical, opera, country, spirituals, hymns

But here's a question: the things I say I love—am I true to them? I am steeped in George MacDonald, fierce nineteenth-century Scottish advocate of God's consuming love. I have read his sermons, novels, and fantasies. Everywhere, he encourages me to ask serious questions about myself, and to live the truth I know. Can I know myself, or probe myself truly, so as to understand the quality of my love? I know I have not been and am not true as I should be, as a child of the Truth. I often say to people, I love such-and-such—as in the list above, but if it is true that I love these things, how is my love borne out or manifested?

Music, for example. I say I love music. What should that mean? To be engaged in it somehow, for a good part of one's time; to do it, to the extent of one's ability, and to grow in that ability; to listen to music, and to learn about what one listens to; to know the heart of it; to learn *why* one loves music—and which music, of all that is available to know, is best, or best-loved.

It appears on reflection that I have *never* loved music thus. I have at times enjoyed music—especially singing—have often delighted in it, as I had the gift of a pretty voice. But enjoyment is mostly superficial. It is not to love—as to know, to enter into, to appreciate what is in a song or a symphony or an opera. I have been only a superficial lover of music. I despised and wasted so much opportunity to be more, learn more, become more. Or, to be truthful, not entirely so. I did enter into choral singing fairly deeply, but still, not usually because of true love of the music, but because of the enjoyment I took from it. And it was easy for me to go pretty far without too much effort. I had a good instrument and a good sense of pitch, and I could sight-read well enough to not have to really learn the music. I coasted along on the surface of it, therefore, and was often praised, which didn't do me any good.

What I have written should lead to repentance. Indeed, I feel an inner grief that I so carelessly treated the gifts and opportunities I was given. But the deeper wrong is to have pretended a love that was not true. Here is an amazing idea: God may have given music to me as a child, as a potential pathway to himself. How much pain I could have spared myself and so many others if I had opened myself and given myself to truly loving the music that was in me and so abundantly available! Even so, I must also acknowledge that God graciously accepted me at the level I could respond to this gift, and I have been truly blessed by it, by music, and by singing, all my life. He didn't, in other words, withdraw the gift because I couldn't fully enter into its potential. He did use it as one means to find out about his love. Music, now, isn't for the same purpose in my life as it might have been when I was young and so badly in need of clear truth and beauty and love. But I praise God for teaching me this truth in my inner being.

So, let me consider music in this light, as a pathway God gave me to find himself. Along that way lay hymns. My folks, intellectuals though they were, loved hymns and spirituals. My dad had a wonderful bass voice, and loved to sing such hopeful and mournful songs as "Deep River," "Swing Low, Sweet Chariot," and "Were You There When They Crucified my Lord?" Mother would sit at the piano, and I and my dad (perhaps my brother, though I don't see him in my memory) would peer over her shoulder at the music on the stand, and sing those hymns. And Christmas carols! Oh my goodness, how we loved those! I dimly realized even as a child that the words to most of them seemed to have at least as much to do with the death of Jesus on the cross as with his birth in a lowly manger. One of my favorites was "O Come, O Come, Emmanuel." I loved the minor mode of the melody, which seemed to match the words:

> O come, O come, Emmanuel, and ransom captive Israel,
> That mourns in lonely exile here
> Until the Son of God appear.
> Rejoice! Rejoice! Emmanuel shall come to thee, O Israel!"[1]

What I couldn't know at the time was how these hymns would have a delayed reaction, and that years later their words would light up for me, recognized and already loved, but finally understood.

1. Jones, *Hymnbook*, 147.

Set in beauty

What other things I loved did God use to prepare me to receive his Son? High on the list, I'm sure, is my love of the natural world. I grew up in such a beautiful place—like a park—outside of Princeton, New Jersey. The house we moved into when I was seven was built before the Revolutionary War, and was the site of one of the crucial battles in that war, the Battle of Princeton. General Mercer, after whom many places in the region were named—including our street—died of battle wounds in our house. The house had been used as a field hospital, and the room in which he died was a tiny corner room where we could still see traces of that battle. The floor was said to have soaked up the dying general's blood, and several battlefield artifacts had been collected and were displayed somewhat casually in that room by my folks. We called it "the Mercer Room." It was also always used as our Christmas tree room. It was just big enough to put a medium-sized tree—always chopped down from somewhere on our property—and the room was closed off to us children until Christmas morning, when we could see the results of Santa's visit.

The acreage surrounding this historic house was gloriously varied: in the front, there was a great sweeping lawn (mostly very bumpy with the up-heaving roots of the many maples, beeches, and other trees that grew there). Beyond that lay a large field owned by someone else, in the middle of which was a huge old oak tree and a monument to the Battle of Princeton. On one side of the house a long drive looped around a barn-type building, which we used as a garage and tool storage space, and there was a loft where our ubiquitous cats always chose to have their kittens. I can almost remember the dark and mysterious smell when a new litter was born.

Behind and beside the house were a smoke house, a pump house for the well, and a wood shed; beyond these lay a small apple orchard and a large field we cultivated—growing all the vegetables our family needed. On the other side of the house, a pathway between crab apple trees and wisteria vines led to a funny old shack that we used as a play house. It was screened in only, but I decided one year that I would sleep there for the whole year. It became mighty cold and damp in the winter, and the pathway was often snowy, but I was determined to show that I could do it! (It's possible I didn't last the whole winter—my memory fades at this point). Once I went with my big brother and his friends on a rare outing to see the movie *Abbott and Costello Meet Frankenstein*. When Dracula was about to rise up from his coffin, I was too scared to look! My brother reassured me it was only a man in a tuxedo. But I was truly terrified by the werewolf—watching Lon Cheney, Jr. slowly change from a man to a wolf was too much for my ten-year-old heart. *And*, I had to walk down the path to that shack to go to bed that night, and of course the moon was full.

Back on the other side beyond the barn/garage, there was a small field where we played touch football at Thanksgiving, and beside which was a chicken house. At one point, we were raising chickens for eggs, and also to eat; we had "layers" and "broilers." I remember the pleasure of going into the chicken house and collecting eggs from the warm nests, although I didn't much like the smell in there. In addition to all this, we had a small hazelnut orchard, with both gooseberry and currant bushes nearby—all of which we harvested in season.

My favorite kind of pie has always been gooseberry, though I have rarely found it since childhood days. Preparing the gooseberries involved a tedious process, which I did *not* enjoy. First, you had to pick them from stiff, low branches, delicately reaching your fingers in between the serious thorns, berry by berry, and I was instructed to be sure to pick *all* of them! Then you had to get them ready for the pie (or the preserves). That entailed picking up each berry and snipping off the little flower tail with your fingernails, a job we carried out on the relatively cool back porch of the house where there was also an outdoor sink. Summers in Princeton were hot and humid. You never could stay dry for very long, even after a cool shower. Starched pinafores wilted the moment I put them on. I always marveled at girls in school, as I got older, who seemed to be unaffected by the heat and looked cool and neat.

This fairy tale house and grounds was my refuge and pleasure—when not pressed into one chore or another. As the middle child separated on one side from my older brother by seven years, and my younger half-sister by five years, I seemed to be on my own most of the time. If I had free time and needed to be indoors—in winter, or at night—there were books in every room; I always had a book going. There was music to play on the record player, or special radio dramas to listen to. But perhaps the best part of our place was the woods just behind our property—owned by the Princeton Institute of Advanced Studies, open to anyone. I spent hours there, explor-ing intriguing paths through mounds of honeysuckle, wading in the brook that flowed through the woods, collecting special stones. The woods were safe, apparently, in those years—1940s and early '50s—and there was never any question about it being OK for me to be in those mysterious depths on my own. Our house (which now has been restored to its pre-Revolutionary War configuration and is called Battlefield Park) was out of town about three miles, so I also spent lazy days riding my bicycle along little traveled country roads, rejoicing in my ability to ride without hands.

I loved the flowers of spring, the earliest ones noted with excitement by all of us: the first bloodroot in the still leafless woods, the fringing of green on the forsythia bushes, the dense golden star-like flowers soon to follow, and the sudden exuberance of apple blossoms, wisteria, lilacs, and peonies. Violets grew tall in the grass under the apple trees, and you could pick great handfuls and put them in special vases on all the windowsills in the house. The trees were steadfast and trustworthy companions. I especially loved the old maples, which were easy to climb. I often took a book up into a tree and read as though in a hideaway.

My dad was a strong influence on my life. He was six-feet, four-inches tall and had a deeply resonant bass voice. I respected him, but was mostly in awe of him. He was distant emotionally; never unkind, he also never took me on his lap or told me he loved me. I think I now know that he couldn't love me, which I will explain. But as a young girl, my father was an important force, mostly for good. He taught me how to dive through the great Atlantic breakers when we vacationed at Fire Island, where friends had a summer cabin. He taught me to fish (and to clean the fish I caught), and to canoe, using a variety of strokes that could keep the canoe smoothly surging across the lake. I always felt he must love me, even though he didn't show it in ways a child needs.

Cruel and loving

But now let me turn to the place where the roots of my faith cross. I grew up without the love of a mother—and, as it turned out, without the love of a father. Before I continue, let me say that this sad lack is so widespread in Rwanda as to be almost the norm—and of course it is elsewhere as well. *Most* young people I know, and know about, in Rwanda either don't know one or the other parent, or grew up in homes lacking in the most basic necessities of a normal life. When these are lacking, and when the remaining parent is also lacking in the experience of being raised lovingly, there is little chance the children will know anything about love. I don't at all wish anyone to think I feel myself to be unique or in need of pity any more than the countless others who also missed the God-ordained blessings of loving and nurturing parents. My story does, however, help me to understand others with similar losses, and also to be able to come alongside them with some word or deed of comfort that others might not be moved to bring.

My mother died soon after I was born, as a result of giving birth to me. I was raised for the first year or so by my dad's youngest sister, and then he remarried. My stepmother was a beautiful and very talented woman. She had enjoyed some success as an actress on Broadway, and my dad managed to lure her away from a promising career. Her name was Moyne, but she had been nicknamed Peter, after Peter Pan, because she had played that role on the stage. She was a superb actress, and her skill in acting played a significant role in shaping my sensibilities, my sense of who I was, and of who she was.

In my youth, her main energies became focused on children's theater; she started a school for children who wanted to learn about theater, which provided an opportunity to learn drama and theater craft through a great range of hands-on experiences. She wrote two books on children's theater, including plays she had created (available still today on Amazon, under Moyne Rice Smith). I participated often in these activities, and our attic was full of old costumes, props, and pieces of stage sets, ready to be mined and recycled in the next venture. She was a great teacher and director. Children loved her, and so did most grown-ups.

The problem was that at home she behaved entirely different than she did in public settings. She could be wonderful at times—loving and eager to create a fun atmosphere, but at other times she would become harsh, and cruelly sarcastic. Her sarcasm was frequent, and aimed primarily at me and my dad. On many occasions—especially as I entered my teens—she would tell me I was a fat slob and would never amount to anything. I remember just once challenging her on this—did she really believe I would never be anything worthwhile? She affirmed that prophecy, though by God's grace it has since been nullified. When the cruel sarcasm was aimed at my dad, he seemed to just absorb it, not in any way fighting back or confronting her, nor ever standing up for me. At the time, I justified his not coming to my defense by telling myself he couldn't, or he would jeopardize his marriage. I was thus without any defense against this sort of cruelty, and I took it all in, deeply. In large part, it shaped who I was, how I saw myself. But because she could also be so apparently loving and creative, I craved and needed those moments from her.

I still fondly remember how good she was at helping me select a new book to read from our very large library at home. She knew all the books as friends, and when I asked her to find me one, she was always ready to show me several selections, telling me about each one. When I was sick (and I was quite ill at times, including a hospital stay for what was diagnosed as "glandular fever"), she was everything a sick child could want. She would make sure I was warm enough, or cool enough, and had what I wanted to eat. She would read to me by my bedside—I loved hearing her read, whether *The Wind in the Willows*, or *Winnie the Pooh*, or *Mary Poppins*— she read engagingly. It's a wonder I didn't become a hypochondriac! In such an inconsistent environment, I was never sure what sort of response I might get from her, and I kept trying to position myself to either avoid her or come at her loving side; I craved her approval, her love.

Perhaps because of this atmosphere growing up, I began to develop various behaviors which only added fuel to Mother's sarcastic fire. For example, I became obsessed with food. I would sneak cookies or candy whenever I could (and would always be found out). We had a big freezer in the basement, where there was a gallon container of vanilla ice cream. I used to bring a spoon down there, and scrape across the top of the ice cream, taking as many bites as I thought I could get away with without the lower level being noticed. When I was in high school, I occasionally stole snacks from a store on the way to school, and I added other behaviors: I started smoking. I began to be very interested in sex (although I didn't find any real opportunities to practice that interest until I left home). I became untrustworthy in a variety of ways.

Surprisingly, I was also doing quite well in school, and because I was a singer, I was involved in all the music programs Princeton High School offered. It was that music program alone that gave me a sense of value and belonging. I was selected as the lead in the Broadway hit *Carousel* when Princeton was the first high school to be permitted to stage that musical. That was a high point for me—my young sister, whom in many ways I looked up to for her discerning spirit, told me that she had cried when I acted the scene where my boyfriend was dying in my lap. I recall I had to whisper my lines—and as anyone in theater knows, it is almost impossible to whisper and be heard all the way out in the audience.

When it came time to think about going to college, out of laziness I chose only one school to apply to—Oberlin College, in Ohio. There were two reasons for choosing this school: it was far away from home, so I would be free of my stepmother, and unlike most other schools, it didn't require college boards. I was accepted on the basis of my grades alone.

Missed opportunities

In college, I had an opportunity to come into myself, as a singer and a person. I had no financial worries, as my dad was paying for my tuition and all expenses. I was out from under the malevolent influence of my stepmother. And I came into contact with students who were Christians. Everything would seem to have been set for a major turnaround and forward progress. This did not happen. Although I "gave my life to Jesus Christ" in the company of these Christian students (and loved the attention I got as a new believer), my life didn't show any effects of that decision. Instead, I began to find ways to express my sexual interests; I cut class often, and began to flunk more courses than I passed. After the first year, it was decided that perhaps I'd do better enrolled in the music program (which would have made sense at the start, but for some reason I began as a liberal arts student), so I began taking both piano and voice lessons. But I never practiced. It's simply not possible to progress musically without discipline and practice.

After two years of mostly wasted opportunity, I made the decision to quit school. I told my dad I'd decided to move to California, which is where my brother lived; I'd hook up with him and see what would happen next. I had no plans at all beyond quitting school. My dad accepted this decision, perhaps relieved, and off I went to California. There, I landed on my brother's doorstep.

3

While Still an Enemy

I HAD PRETTY MUCH idolized my big brother when he was at home. He left for university when I was ten, and it was a huge loss for me; he was my only ally against my stepmother. He hated her, and his parting words to me were that I should also hate her. (Fortunately for my spirit, I couldn't do so.) It was my brother who explained the facts of life to me, using a helpful book with good illustrations. I have no idea where he found that book! I always felt he would look out for me, so he was an obvious refuge when I didn't know where else to turn after leaving college.

I overstayed my welcome by several months, showing no inclination to move on with my life. Finally, my brother kindly offered to help me get unstuck. I was then very overweight (food was still very much an issue), and he offered to take me to a weight doctor, and to get me settled in an apartment on my own. The weight doctor's regimen worked, and I lost weight. I found an apartment and a job fairly quickly, and began to feel that I was somebody. I was now quite attractive in my new body, and I loved to dress seductively and wear high heels to work. I began dating, and before long, I met my husband. He was my neighbor in our apartment duplex, and we took to each other quickly. He was married, but separated, and planning on divorce. Very soon we began to live together, planning to marry as soon as he would be free.

That marriage was wrong from the beginning. I had no idea of who I was, much less how to be a wife and mother. From the start, I continued to flirt with other men. My husband was a workaholic, and I spent much of the early years alone, trying to raise my three daughters who came along fairly quickly. I was trying to be a good mom, but I didn't know anything about parenting. I would read books and try to adopt their advice, but never felt it was resonating with who I was. I was often neglectful and impatient with my girls, while also loving them as well as I could. We lived near the ocean in Manhattan Beach, California, and it was a relief to take them to the beach because then they could play freely without my having to constantly tell them "no!"

The worst decision

During the late 1960s, when society was turning inside out and upside down, I became involved with whatever movement was going: I joined something called the Indian Land and Life Society (whose mission was for non-native Americans to team up with Native Americans (still called "Indians" at that time) to help them submit legal briefs to regain lost land titles). I campaigned for equal rights. I "sat in" on demonstrations (at first called "love-ins") with my family in the park. We became, for all intents and purposes, a hippie family. I began to drink a lot, and tried pot. I wasn't happy with the way I felt on dope—too out of control—but somehow that state was tolerable when induced by alcohol. My brother was a heavy drinker, and we would often drink together, commiserating on our marriages, neither of which was doing well.

At that time, I began a prison visiting program with some friends, and I found myself falling for a man I had met there. By the time he was released, we had conspired together that I should go away with him, leaving my family behind. It's hard now, even for me, to understand how this could have happened. I know I wasn't in love with him, nor he with me—but we were strongly attracted. I allowed myself to get caught up in what seemed like "romance"; I managed to convince myself that I couldn't live without Herman. He, a very charming but unscrupulous man, convinced me that he wanted me to be with him. What was really going on was a simple but dangerous flirtation. I was vulnerable as the wife of a workaholic and emotionally unavailable husband. I had already given myself up to many of the prevailing ideas of the era, such as "if it feels good, do it." The spirit of the age was amazingly permissive, promiscuous, amoral—while at the same time somehow invigorating because of all the political and social upheavals. There was Bob Dylan, and the Beatles, and an endless stream of others promoting sexual freedom and other "freedoms" from the "establishment" that had us all bound. I was a ready and available, and willing, victim. I plotted with Herman to leave with him when he was released from prison (the charge was forgery, by the way); though I could hardly stand the thought of leaving my daughters, it seemed to me I must do this, and so I did.

This was the single worst decision of my life; I left my three girls— aged seven, eight, and ten—without a mother. I left them at the mercy of a distraught father who also had become caught up in the spirit of the age, and was behaving irresponsibly as a parent—and, I learned later, abusively. The myriad consequences of that decision have reverberated through all our lives from that moment until now.

In cruel irony, that relationship with Herman failed its own dubious promise; it lasted only a year and a half. It was never a good relationship. Herman was black, and we lived in a black community in San Francisco— at first, in Marin City, in a high-rise complex that was notorious for its crime and police absence. His sister hated me. His friends mostly were content to ignore me, as long as Herman was available to drink with them. I tried desperately to fit in, to be accepted, but since I had not yet found out who or what I was—what sort of a life I wanted, or what sort of person I wanted to be—I was mostly just sidelined. After a while, I became seri- ously concerned about Herman's drinking, and I decided to leave him. My oldest daughter had come to live with us by this time, my husband having declared her "unmanageable." I had become fearful that he might become violent in his now-evident alcoholism. My daughter and I fled in secret, helped by a friend across the Bay, and I moved back to the Los Angeles area where my other daughters and ex-husband still lived. Now, with my deeply damaged preteen daughter, I tried to somehow put my life together, while still being unchanged within.

I had continued to maintain contact with my two girls who remained with their father and stepmother. He had married a woman who provided a very emotionally unstable home for them, and who had, like me, left her husband and children to marry him. While still with Herman, I drove from San Francisco to Los Angeles to visit them about once a month. We were always happy to be together, and it was terribly hard to part again. But even after leaving Herman, I was still very much into myself, not really caring about their needs, or anyone else's.

Through it all, there were persistent reminders of God. At various points along the "road . . . that leads to destruction" (Matt 7:13) I would suddenly feel the need to go into an empty church. More than once, I attended evangelistic meetings and "came forward" to receive Jesus as my Lord and Savior. But on the other hand, I would energetically argue with Christians (who seemed always to be around) who wanted to talk to me about Christianity. I was proud of my ability to refute all their claims. Truly, I was mixed up, deep within.

Surprise invitations

God worked in a mysterious way to draw me to seek him. When I was still with Herman, he surprised me one day by asking me to go to church with him. He had never before mentioned that he had any interest in church. I was surprised, too, by my response: I wanted to go, and during the service I felt a strong inner response. Afterwards, I asked the pastor if I could meet with him the next day. All I can remember of that conversation in his office is that I cried while he talked, because I knew that he was talking about what I badly wanted, but I could understand nothing he said; he may as well have been speaking a foreign language. I returned to my life with no apparent change; this encounter seemed to have no effect on me at all.

Now, living on my own with my oldest daughter, I had found a good job in the San Francisco Bay area—we were living in Mountain View. (God was very gracious in this; I never lacked a job in all this confused time.) One day, I found myself responding positively to a coworker's invitation to church. Looking back, it seems as if I had a sign on my forehead which only certain people could read: "Invite me to church!" Between these two invitations, I cannot recall that I had any thoughts of God or church—other than to argue with whoever wanted to discuss Christianity with me. But here I was, again going eagerly to church, expecting something to happen. You see? There was a change in me: I was looking for something. At the end of the service, however, I felt let down; I thanked my host for inviting me, but told him I hadn't found what I was looking for—whatever that was.

And now the move of God was on. This friend kindly suggested another church he thought I might like—a special Sunday evening service called "Body Life." I went there, to Peninsula Bible Church in Palo Alto, the next week, on my own. And there, the veil of my unbelief began to be lifted, as I heard passages from the Bible being taught in a powerful, easy to understand, and very appealing manner. It was my first exposure to what is called expository Bible teaching, and it was like fresh water to my long-parched spirit. That Body Life service was a child of its time, within what became known as the "Jesus movement." The large church was totally filled with people. The "service" —not at all conventional, in normal church terms—involved a fine exposition of a portion of the Bible (which they carried on sequentially—teaching a whole book of the Bible before going on to another), followed by a period of sharing. There were guys with portable mics, and the leader invited anyone to share from their experience—either something they had learned from the Word, or some new awareness they had come to as a Christian, or a struggle, or a need. When someone expressed a need, the leader called upon a person in the audience to go right away to pray for that person. It was orderly, but with also a sense of the Spirit of God's presence. The offering was done in an unusual way: people were invited to share what they could—giving their offering—but also people were invited to *take* from the offering plate if they had need. I've not seen this done anywhere else since.

After only a few weeks, I think, of going to this church and listening to the teaching of the many competent pastors (led by Ray Stedman) I was surrounded by Christians who told me they were praying for me. I read C. S. Lewis' *Mere Christianity*, and by the end, I felt I had no leg left for my unbelief to stand on. I admired C. S. Lewis greatly. I saw him as an intellectual, as I considered myself to be. If such a one as he was a believer, that convinced me. Soon afterwards, I gave in, gave up, and recognized Jesus as my Savior and my Lord. I say "recognized" because I now believe he had been there in me for years, while I fought and resisted and went my own way. Now at last I could see him there, and I could give myself to him, let him take over. While I was still an enemy of Christ, opposing him at every opportunity, he graciously pursued and won me to full acceptance of his love and saving grace.

That was in 1972, and I was thirty-six years old. Just recently I told a friend that I always think of myself as thirty-six (at this writing, my chronological age is eighty). She wondered if thirty-six was my age when I started following Christ. And of course, it was! Until that moment, I had just thought of my inner self—my eternal self—as age thirty-six. It seemed a nice age to be—mature but still in my prime. But it was also the age I became a new person in Christ. From that beginning of a long conversion, I immersed myself in the Word of God, and studied to be a Bible teacher. At Peninsula Bible Church, they offered a two-year "Scribe School" that included two years of Greek, one year of Hebrew, and such courses as Christology, church history, introduction to Old and New Testaments, and hermeneutics. It was a rigorous program, and I am sure God used it to prepare me for all the subsequent teaching I did.

Most important, I now began the long road of making amends and seeking forgiveness from those I had harmed in my years of running my life on self. While I carried out the major tasks in this process, I was enfolded and nurtured by a small group—we called it a house church—of dedicated young Christians who were serious about seeking and doing God's will. We met weekly for Bible study, singing and worship, sharing our lives and questions, and a potluck meal. We grew up together in Christ. We held each other accountable, caring more for each other's spiritual growth and well-being than for being nice to each other.

Discipleship begins

Once, after I had been in the group for some time, I slipped back into a relationship with a man I had been seeing before my conversion. One result of this was that I absented myself from the fellowship of the group—in particular of my best friend in that group. Darkness has no fellowship with the light, I discovered. After a short time, my friend called me, and strongly rebuked me. Though I had not told her what I was doing, she could discern that I was trying to hide something from her and the others, and knowing my story, she had a good idea what was going on. I am very thankful to God that I was able to accept her rebuke and remove myself from that ungodly relationship, and to be restored to the precious fellowship that nothing else on this earth can equal.

Also during these first years of learning to be a Christian I was most fortunate to enter what amounted to a spiritual mentor program with none other than Pastor Ray Stedman. I was put on staff at Peninsula Bible Church as editor of Ray's sermon series, which I was to fashion into books—one of which was the very well-known and popular *Body Life*. (This book has been reissued with the subtitle: *The Book That Inspired a Return to the Church's Real Meaning and Mission.)*

My job was to edit the sermons and shape them into chapters for a book. I would remove dated references, repetitions from one sermon to another, and other extraneous material that wouldn't be understood by the general public. In the process, I read my Bible along with Ray. He preached through the Bible, never topically, so I read with him, trying to understand everything he said in interpretation and application of the biblical texts.

There were occasions when I would not be able to see how he made a particular conclusion from the text, and I would flag those spots. Then at our weekly conferences, I would bring these up, asking him if he could make it clearer. He was always most gracious and humble in the face of what might well have seemed inexcusable cheek on my part. Here I was, a brand new Christian posing interpretation questions to the great Ray Stedman! But he never gave me any impression other than kindly interest. Occasionally he would laugh and acknowledge that he couldn't explain how he had arrived at a certain understanding or insight. In these sessions—as in all the many, many sermon series I edited into books—I received an invaluable blessing and foundation for my Christian faith.

The worst decision I ever made has plowed through my life, and that of my daughters and others, leaving a great deal of damage and wreckage. The best decision I ever made, to turn my life over to Christ and try to serve and know him, was the start of an amazing redemptive process—a long, and continuing process—which has shown me the truth of the prophecy: "I will repay you for the years the locusts have eaten—the great locust and the young locust, the other locusts and the locust swarm—my great army that I sent among you. You shall eat in plenty and be satisfied, and praise the name of the Lord your God, who has dealt wondrously with you. And my people shall never again be put to shame." (Joel 2:25–26)

4

Hearing God's Voice

It is a continuing wonder to me that God communicates with his people. From the time of Adam and Eve, throughout the Bible, God shares his thoughts and plans with his people. The fact that our transcendent, Creator God desires to let us hear his voice strongly illustrates his humility. The Bible says, "in these last days, God has spoken to us by his Son" (Heb 1:2). It was Jesus, humbling himself to become a man, who clearly communicated God's love to all people, and to each one who desires to know him. Over the years since I began to follow Jesus, I have heard his voice (speaking clear words to my inner ear) several times. I share them with the desire to honor God and to encourage readers. One strong thing I have come to know is that God is faithful to lead his children.

The first time I heard his voice was when I turned over my life to him. At that time, he gave me two clear injunctions: I was to be sexually pure from then on, and I was to accept the Scriptures in the Bible as his word, inspired and coming from him. As to the first, I had to stumble once before I grasped the importance of abstaining from sex—and that stumble communicated clearly to me that the Spirit of God had come to live in me; sexual offense was a grief to the Spirit of God, and I felt that grief.

As for the second, I understood that I was not to pick and choose among the Scriptures—which ones I would believe, or agree with, and which I would set aside. I knew that I would not always understand what I read, and that I would have many questions, but I was to maintain that foundational belief that all of God's word *was* God's word. That has anchored my faith in a profound way. I have wandered in and out of various themes and fashions of theology, in which the Bible comes under fire from many scholars. The basic assumption God insisted on at the time of my conversion has enabled me to examine these ideas, seeking to understand them, while retaining my confidence in the wholly inspired word of God. I am in the so-called conservative camp regarding the inspiration of the Bible. I believe it is all "God-breathed," and all of it is, or can be, instructive to our lives as followers of Christ.

Not far into my journey with Christ, I heard another word from God, compelling a major change in my habits. I was a smoker, and had been since my teenage years. Though smoking had by 1972 become an increasingly anti-social act, banned in many public places, I persisted with my nearly three-pack-a-day habit. One day I was on a long trip, driving from Northern California where I lived, to Los Angeles to visit my daughters. As I drove along, I decided to have a cigarette. When I began to light up, I clearly heard God say, "Am I your Lord or not?" That was all, but I knew beyond any doubt that he wanted me to settle the question of who or what was Lord, what would control my life. Smoking had a firm grip on me—the habit had the upper hand and ordered me about mercilessly. I had to decide, then and there, if Jesus truly was Lord in my life, *my* Lord, or not. It was not difficult to decide. There is something about knowing that it is God himself who is speaking to you, personally, that seems to just eliminate all other ideas or choices, all arguments. I told him yes; he is my Lord. I threw out the cigarette and didn't return to smoking, though it was not easy. As anyone who has had that habit knows, it can be very, very tough to break. I thought about smoking in connection with almost every action I took during the day, from first thing on awaking in the morning, to the last thing at night. But I had that word from God: Am I your Lord, or not?

Some years later, while I was in graduate school working on a PhD in English, I again heard God's clear voice. I was fond of drinking wine at that time—had been for a long time. I chose restaurants for lunch on the basis of whether they served wine. I kept a large jug of wine in my fridge, and that was the first place I went when I came home—to pour a glass of wine, and to drink it thirstily like water, followed by another and another. I often went to bed in a very fuzzy state. There were also times when I drove after drinking too much.

One night I awoke around midnight, and felt that it somehow seemed very dark, more than just because it was night; there was a spiritual atmosphere of darkness. In that moment, I heard God say, "You are an alcoholic, and you need to get help." Nothing subtle or needing interpretation—it couldn't have been clearer. Because I knew it *was* God, I knew what he said was true, and the next day I was ready to begin what turned out to be a long and very wonderful journey with Alcoholics Anonymous. I had not ever considered that I might be an alcoholic, but I had God's word for it, so I chose not to question it.

God brought me into that fellowship, which is based firmly on the importance of finding a "higher power"—though I was already a Christian—to teach me things I wouldn't otherwise have thought I needed to know. For the first time, I saw myself as someone who needed community. I was not meant to live in isolation, as I had been doing. And God brought me into contact with an amazing and diverse group of people, many of whom became friends. Some I helped on their way to sobriety, and others helped me. There were guys in ties, and punks, and smelly homeless folks, and jittery teenagers, and worn-out men and women who had "hit bottom," yet tried every conceivable way to get out of acknowledging alcohol's grip on their lives. There were gays and homophobes, Christians and atheists. Truly, AA is a microcosm of the society of the world. And God wanted me to become one of *them*. It was amazing how quickly I took to the program and the fellowship. In church, I often found myself longing for the kind of honesty and sharing we had in AA meetings. I saw many people healed by the love of God mediated through that fellowship and through the powerful and wise Twelve Steps. My Christianity could only deepen and thrive in such a setting. I went to the same meeting every day for years. People came and went, but again and again I felt humbled by the kind of truth and transparency I found there.

In all these instances of hearing God's voice, the results have been remarkable and lasting changes in me and in my life circumstances, all stemming from obedience and the follow-up of a faithful God who is determined to make me like Jesus.

5

Invitation to Rwanda

WITHOUT A DOUBT, THE most life-changing words I have ever heard from God, since I started to follow Jesus, came in 2004. To provide the full context, let me tell about my first trip to Rwanda. Early in 2003, after reading yet another full-page spread in the newspaper focusing on some dire issue in Africa, it occurred to me to wonder if my church was considering any kind of outreach or missionary activity in that continent. After inquiring, I found that there were two women who had been praying about this very question for some time, and I decided to join them. Over the course of many months, our prayer group grew—we called it Alongside Africa—and we determined after considerable research and prayer that Rwanda would be the country to focus on. I was serving as prayer coordinator for this group, and as our information and interest grew, so did our conviction that we should send a team to Rwanda.

We had made contact with the team leader of African Evangelistic Enterprise (AEE)-Rwanda, Antoine Rutayasire, and we also had met the charismatic and warm founder of African Enterprise, Michael Cassidy. AEE-Rwanda was then preparing for the tenth anniversary of the 1994 genocide, and the plan emerged that our team should come alongside AEE in this major city-wide evangelistic outreach in July of 2004, when the annual one-hundred-day memorial period would be wrapping up.

While the team formed itself—one after another person committing to going—I continued to pray, and wonder what I should do. I ended up going, but it was not clear to me that this was what God wanted. I seemed to myself to be just following along with everyone else. I had indeed been integral to the planning and prayer leading up to this trip, and I'm sure the others had no doubt I should go, but I was still uncertain even as I stepped on that plane—heading for Africa! For me, it was the first time I had ever been to a developing, or third-world, country.

We had a great team, and AEE did an amazing job of coordinating the complexities of a city-wide mission, including what they call stratified evangelism. They included us total greenhorns, who knew almost nothing of the culture or people of Rwanda, into their plans, folding us into all the activities. In the mornings, we were driven to a very large permanent tent to attend meetings where pastor training was being carried out. In the afternoons, we went in pairs to various local ministries—street kids, prostitutes, cooperatives, AEE self-help groups—to observe, preach, give testimonies, and pray for the people. In the evenings, we were sent out in triads to different churches where the key evangelists of AE International were preaching. They had come from Ghana, Kenya, South Africa, Burundi, Uganda, Tanzania, Congo, Belgium, United States, Canada, and the United Kingdom. Our people were given three tasks: one person was to record the outcome of the evangelistic appeal, another was to give a personal testimony, and the third was to spend the time praying. Night after night, we did this—a different church each night, rotating tasks among us. We heard powerful messages from the evangelists and personal testimonies from our own people that delighted and moved all of us.

As the days went on, it became apparent that God had indeed intended that I go along. My team members and I couldn't help observing a remarkable phenomenon: each day, sometimes more than once, I found myself in deep, heart-to-heart communication with a different Rwandese person. I knew no Kinyarwanda, and only a little French (but in general only the educated people speak French, so that was not much use). Yet there I was, connecting with one person after another. One day, one of my team members asked me, "So, Jean, do you still feel you weren't supposed to come on this trip?" I had to admit that something was quite evidently going on that I was getting to be a part of, orchestrated by God.

By the end of that trip, I had made several connections with people with whom I later developed relationships of various kinds. Although I didn't know it at the time, it was a sort of seed-planting process, the "seeds" being the people, whom God would eventually bring to harvest.

Returned to the United States, I was in the post-mission-trip throes of reflection and prayer, accompanied by frequent tears and a very strong love for Rwanda and its people. I was immersed in Scripture, probably more than I ever had been before. As I prayed, wept, and wondered what was happening to me, I realized that the heart-pain I was experiencing was what people referred to as a "burden"; I had come back with a burden for Rwanda. That amazed me. I don't think I had ever felt that way about a country or a people before.

One day while in personal devotions I heard God's voice—at least I knew it wasn't coming from me—saying these exact words: "You could go and live there." As I look back on that moment, I think I knew immediately that it was God himself, inviting me to go to Rwanda, but in such a way as to require me to examine the idea thoroughly, and to discern whether or not it was truly him calling me. It was a gentle word of invitation, and it ushered in a period of unprecedented searching, questioning, doubting, and wondering.

I know now that my memory has created a tidy package of what happened during that time, but looking into my journals, I see the reality. On the one hand, my memory tells me that from that moment, I went forward confidently, asking my pastor, my teammates, my friends, and my daughters what they thought of this novel idea, and that all of them confirmed or approved of the plan. My memory tells me that I then returned to God, as he was waiting for my reply, and I told him I'd go if it was truly him sending/inviting me. Then, my memory says, I went about my preparations in a matter-of-fact way, having totally settled the question in my mind about going to Rwanda to live.

Memory, as I said at the outset, is very tricky. Although what I remember is not exactly wrong, it fails to bring in the rather messy and even wearisome details of what was actually a long, drawn-out process of seeking God's confirmation. Apparently, I needed to go through that, as is evident from excerpts from my journal.

> Prayer for Rwanda, beloved country. God has given me *such* love for the people, the country. This is so much more than I had imagined it would be—not just one of the things I'm involved in, but my heart is captured.
>
> I ask God to shape my emotions and to protect me in them, my vulnerable aspect, where his strength can be made perfect. I value the tears that come as I pray, but cannot use feelings as a sure guide—only God's word.

Flooded with tears of desire and longing and joy in the Lord. That he would burn me up in his love, that there would be nothing left of me. The wave recedes. The cat sleeps soundly at the other end of the couch; a crow's cry punctuates the quiet of the morning.

"For the king trusts in the Lord, and through the steadfast love of the Most High he shall not be moved" (Ps 21:7 NRSV). Keep my eyes away from the circumstances and questions and fears, and trained on you, your purpose, and the people of Rwanda. "O my God, I trust in thee: let me not be ashamed, let not mine enemies triumph over me" (Ps 25:2 KJV).

My heart is weighed down with something—don't know what. I turn to the Lord; what is this? Later: a mighty surge of feeling came over me as I began again to think about going to Rwanda—to live and work there. Is this God moving me? Me longing for something I imagine is in Rwanda and not here? My life here is fine, but empty of real passion. There is a great hole to be filled, I seem to realize, which I wasn't aware of before. And I do *not* want to just *fill* it—as with reading, movies, this and that. Even though I'm involved in many activities, when it comes down to time spent, there is a lot left over, and I am not motivated to do much of anything during that time. A hole to be filled.

I am seeking God's direction and hear the words of the song, "Is it I, Lord? I will go, Lord, if you lead me." I think of the Scripture, "For in Christ Jesus . . . the only thing that counts is faith expressing itself through love" (Gal 5:6). I may need to find an English-as-a-second-language course. If God *is* leading me, I can do some things to test that and to prepare. I've found some books to give me more background on Africa and Rwanda. I've made an appointment with my missions pastor to let him know what I'm thinking about, and to ask for his prayer and counsel. I *almost* sense the Lord waiting for *me* to assent. I've asked him to please reveal his will—at least a part–so I can know he's the prime mover here. Later: I have talked to several people, all say moving to Rwanda seems logical, right, not surprising. But you, Lord? It is your confirmation I ask for. But then I wonder, what would make me sure I had it? There have already been many strong indications. I distrust myself, my emotions, is the trouble. Lord, you know; please lead me further.

It should be evident from these few bits from my journal that I was not easy to convince! My very patient Lord needed to feed me abundantly from his word, as I continued to beseech him about this call, until I could take the necessary steps of obedience and faith. It was *much* more difficult than I remembered!

There did come a point where I was able to decide—that was on August 26, 2004, a little over a month after returning from the trip to Rwanda. Here is the journal entry:

> "I removed the burden from their shoulders; their hands were set free from the basket" (Ps 81:6). I understand this speaks of God's release, so as to be able to do God's will and enter into the land. My hands were indeed freed from the necessity of earning a living [I was retired]. Then Ps 116:12: "What shall I return to the Lord for all his goodness to me?" This was the Kigali mission theme. Is this now for me to consider in deciding to go to Rwanda? *Lord, I will go, if you lead and send me.* It is decided, on my end. The way and process are in God's hands. I know the Lord will meet me in all my fears and weakness. He has shown me this abundantly. "O Lord, I am your servant; I am your servant, the child of your serving girl" (Ps 116:16 NRSV).

From that point on, I was on the way, but still earnestly seeking God for his strong leading. I received much encouragement from his word. In October, I read Ps 113:7: "He raises the poor from the dust and lifts the needy from the ash heap." I wrote in response: "I realize that my greatest joy is in encouraging others to hope and trust in God. This is my part in accomplishing the goal of raising up the poor and needy. It seems far removed from what is so desperately needed—renewal of hearts of those in power and position to physically and materially raise the poor up—but without such encouragement, people falter and fail. And who knows, I may be in some chain where power to help may be influenced."

The process I entered into was complex, but clearly orchestrated by God. I was advised by my mission pastor to select a "sending team" to help me think through and carry out all the logistics of getting me to Rwanda. The names of nine people came quickly to mind as I pondered who could help me in this way, and everyone I asked agreed to serve. The process would entail getting my little mobile home on the market, dealing with all my furniture, books, and treasures, selling my car, arranging for living arrangements and good connections in Rwanda, and many other things. During that time, I attended the Perspectives on the World Christian Movement course (see http://www.perspectives.org), which helped me enormously to realize how narrow my worldview had been, and to see the very obvious and consistent emphasis God makes throughout the Bible on the "nations"—his heart has always been in what we call "missions," but I had never seen that before.

Getting ready also involved taking care of my cat. But God arranged to end her life before I left. She had been failing for some time, but seemed to continue to enjoy being with me, and she gave me sweet companionship and fellowship during my prayer times. But a time came when I realized I had to help her to leave this world. She was, an experienced friend told me, only hanging on for me. The day of taking her to the vet and watching her life leave her body is indelible in my memory. I believe with all my heart that I will see her again in the new Earth and new Heaven.

Giving up my house was also much more difficult than I remembered. In the latter part of my stay in Rwanda, I was rummaging through a trunk searching for old journals, and came across color photos from the real estate agency of the listing for my house. As I looked at those pictures, I felt a grief of loss well up in me, which surprised me greatly. Then, as I reread my journal of that time, I saw that giving up this little house had required many efforts to let it go, releasing it to God, only to find it still had an emotional hold on me.

> "I will offer in his tent sacrifices with shouts of joy" (Ps 27:6 NRSV). *What sacrifices shall I offer?* Lord, help me to be truly joyful in all my offerings to you. Let your joy be in me. May I offer my home and way of life here to you *with joy*? I have been feeling sad to give these things up—but if I am offering them to you, how can I be sad? All things are from you, through you, and to you (see Rom 11:36). As you have set me on the Rock so that I am lifted up above all my enemies, so let me be joyful in all my offerings. Change, transform my heart, Lord. With you, all things are possible.
>
> Good Friday: "My God, my God, why have you forsaken me?" (Ps 22:1). I am still, again, feeling the pain of *my* sacrifice—my small offering to God, of my house. It is real pain—and therefore, real sacrifice. The joy is "set before me," perhaps not experienced in the moment, or process, of bringing it. But God has promised, in Jesus' words, to be with me always.
>
> God is meeting me and gentling me through the process of getting ready to put my house—*his* house—on the market. Praise God in whom I live and move and have my being. He is my strength. "Praise be to the Lord, to God our Savior, who daily bears our burdens" (Ps 68:19).

As the months of preparation unfolded—amidst my normal activities (providing spiritual direction, volunteering at a women's shelter, going to exercise/dance classes) God continued to meet me again and again when my emotions threatened to undo me and take away my confidence. In April (about three months before my departure), this was my state of mind/heart:

> Yesterday, and still some today, I was rocked with emotions of, probably, fear—a sense of the bottom falling out. Will God sustain me and see me through—all the way to Rwanda? And be my companion and strength there? And can I get my mind off of *me*, and into the space where God is, loving and longing for the welfare of his people (me and the Rwandans)? Heal my self-centeredness, Lord. Draw my focus to yourself—glorify yourself in me if you can find the way to do that. That is your purpose, that I should live for the praise of your glory. Later: A very strong sense of attack as I stood firm in the strength of his might, focusing all my energy and prayer on the full armor of God, and wielding the Sword with intensity as maybe never before. Brought safely through to praise and worship and a quiet heart.

My last weeks were filled with special times with my daughters, friends, AA group, church members, and my sending team. I was surrounded and sustained and encouraged beyond any possible expectation or hope. I remained fearful and uncertain off and on, but the Lord continued to feed me with Scriptures of encouragement, hope, and promises to lead and sustain me.

> *June 10.* Cut off now from email, phone to be cut off on Monday. Tomorrow I move all remaining things to [daughter] Xan's. Feeling the beginnings of the appalling nature of what I'm doing. Trusting that God is *always* with me—strengthening me and leading me. Everyone says how wonderful it is, what I'm doing. Not feeling wonderful at the moment. Just believe, now. Psalm 25—The whole psalm is what I need now.

In my last week in the states, I was physically weak, with congestion in my chest. My last journal entry before arriving in Kigali has this: "Where is the Lord? Why do I feel no peace or presence?" So much for my memory that all went smoothly from the moment I agreed with God to go and live in Rwanda until the time I got on the plane! How very patient and loving God is!

Before I turn to the Rwanda experience, and try to show some of the ways God worked his mysterious and myriad transformations in me there, I feel that I must look more closely at that preparation time, with particular emphasis on the leading of God through his word. For this I rely on my journal.

6

Led into God's Calling

FROM AUGUST 2004 THROUGH July 2005 when I left for Rwanda, I was seeking, listening, hearing, faltering, fumbling, and being lifted up and restored by God through his word. What follows is a selection of journal entries that record a particular instance of God's words or leading. An unfortunate gap exists, of course, between experienced moments of insight and passion and the written record. At times, I could only give an impression, after the fact, of what had happened in my prayer time.

August 8. Ps 103: I am flooded with the sense of Jesus' loving presence as I praise him, and truly my whole being is lifted in grateful worship, washed with love for him, my God, my Lord, my Father, my Husband, my Friend. He is what I want—only him. He never insists on his own way, however. This strikes me as powerfully true and amazing—that God would be so humble and meek as not to impose himself on me in any way. But how gloriously dear and present he has been to me this morning as I turned to him—so welcoming, embracing, loving. Bless the Lord, O my soul—let *all* that is within me bless his holy name!

Yesterday I disengaged from God, sought the company of self instead. Dreary! My whole joy is in *him*, and my ability and desire to be a blessing to others is only from him. Without him I am like dry weeds.

August 11. In England, one sees signs for entrance and exit, which say, "Way In" and "Way Out." It occurred to me that Jesus is the Way In—to life that is sweet and full and meaningful—and the Way Out of self and all forms of wasted life.

August 15. A glimpse, in chapter 5 of Mark, of Jesus' complete humanity. He was touched by someone, and knew power had gone out from him, as an anonymous woman was healed. My attention has just now been drawn by the Holy Spirit to Jesus' experience. He did not know who had touched him—he needed to ask. He was fully human. He knew and did *only* what the Father revealed and did in him. The Father had done a work, here, without Jesus' volition. I feel awed and privileged to be shown this—a curtain drawn aside. "Who touched me?"

[One of the strong threads in this witness is about my relationship with my daughters—my prayers for them, and the ways God worked to heal and bring about deep repentance, based on true grief because of the harm I did to them—so I include occasional journal entries about them. This was part of the path of preparation to go to Rwanda.]

Another glimpse: As I prayed for my children, I sensed powerfully that what Jesus promised is *true*—that whatever I ask in his name, he will do. As I believed he was praying in me, there was no doubt he would "answer" these prayers. Mystery and wonder.

August 18. Ps 4:3: "Know that the Lord has set apart his faithful servant for himself; the Lord hears when I call to him." Faithful. You, God, are faithful. You are forbearing, patient, kind to me. Help me to be faithful, to mirror your faithfulness, mimicking what you do, in the same way as I tried to mirror the dancing worshipers in Rwanda, until it becomes my dance.

August 30. God speaks this word right to my heart. When I get off in my focus and become "stupid and ignorant," the psalmist says, "Yet I am always with you; you hold me by my right hand. You guide me with your counsel, and afterward you will take me into glory. Whom have I in heaven but you? And earth has nothing I desire besides you" (Ps 73:23–25).

September 1. In prayer, the Lord has brought me to these things this morning concerning Rwanda: that though this is very big, it's just one life, not a world-shattering event. Just me. Humility is essential. That my heart is in process of being tuned more to his—purified of motives other than pure desire to love God and do his will and to show and be love to Rwanda. More, my prayer/his prayer is to give me love for the Rwandan people based more on their needs than on the desire for loving relationship. A heart that will break for them. Nothing of self. A very tall order, Lord! A daily process, too.

He also showed me that he beautifully disposes the members of his body according to his purpose and their gifts, which he helps the body to discern in each other—not by taking a class, but by working together with him *in* the body for the purpose for which he has drawn us together. Out of that common purpose and committed work, and attentiveness to the moving of the Spirit, gifts emerge, perfectly suited for the particular work at hand. Also, it's good that we do not fully see our own gifts—saves us from the need to try to perform according to some idea of what such a gift looks like. At bottom, we need always to put ourselves at Jesus' disposal, and trust him to reveal what is needed—or not—but to use us in his service.

Perspective: "He comes to judge the earth" (Ps 96:13). Do in me, Lord, what you want to do, to give me a *holy urgency*, to do all I'm supposed to and can, in my small or large individual role—as you work in me—to hasten your coming.

September 3. Ps 25:1–2—my theme for these days—and the whole Psalm is pure encouragement. Wait for God, keep eyes on him, and enemies will not prevail. I don't need to watch where I'm going, only look to God, and "he will pluck my feet out of the net." I *can't* see all the possible pitfalls or land mines, but he can. Trust him.

Aline, my Rwandan friend, sends counsel: wait for the timing of God's sending, which I want to do—though there is some impatience. Wait. Lord, I will wait. I realize it's not impatience so much as a desire to go forward so as not to lose momentum with the desire—but that is self, not God. So, wait.

Lord, I want to go to Rwanda, *if* you send me. It would be such joy. Teach me to wait and listen, and fill me with love for Rwanda, more and more. I recommit my heart, my life, my purpose and hopes to you, God. Burn out of me all pride and all self-rising. I wondered if announcing my sense of calling to Rwanda to everyone was premature or foolish—and then thought it was like an engagement announcement: the commitment is made, and the time of fulfillment is in the future, but sure, as God arranges things for his glory. That doesn't mean I'm sure I will go to Rwanda—just sure of my commitment to God and of his wisdom in directing me however he will.

A friend in Rwanda writes that I need to allow time for God to prepare me, as he prepared Moses. I realize that I'm *not* prepared, and that only God knows how to do that. I am in a naive state about what I might do there, and must let God deal with me until his purpose becomes clear.

September 12. Rather bleak. Feels like all my faith and response to God is being questioned. I do not sustain my focus, and it slips off, like a misplaced axe blow, and where am I? Where is God, and my contact with him? Fantasy, foolishness, based on lack of center in myself—it seems. Let

God be God. . . . I need to be willing to stay in the place of humiliation as long as God chooses for me to be here. Things to learn here, and nowhere else. Exaltation must be anchored to humiliation of self, flesh. I sensed, in reading a poem of Wendell Berry, an uneasiness, a disturbance apparently stemming from his treatment of life and death as springing out of each other, and my unwillingness to experience or acknowledge the death part of life. But it's integral.

I remembered that Satan is always prowling, that his attacks on me are spins of the truth—to get me to think either that I am superior because of giftedness *or* inferior because of foolishness or fleshliness. Truth in both extremes: I am gifted—by God, for his glory and the building of his kingdom, by his hand and determination. And I am foolish and fleshly—but all my sin and weakness is no match for God's grace and mercy. He causes me to stand on the Rock, no better than anyone else, and equally deserving of death because of sin, with everyone else. Satan cleverly tries to get *self* into honest examination, so that it becomes self-loathing, and then, God-doubting. With God's help, I am not "ignorant of his schemes."

September 15. I ordered and today received Gerald May's *The Dark Night of the Soul*, which explores the benefits and blessings of this experience of darkness (which he says should be demystified) which comes throughout life to everyone. The book is derived from the writings of John of the Cross and Teresa of Avila.

> If we really knew what we were called to relinquish on this journey, our defenses would never allow us to take the first step. Sometimes the only way we can enter the deeper dimensions of the journey is by being unable to see where we are going. . . . To guide us toward the love that we most desire, we must be *taken* where we could not and would not go on our own.[1]

September 22. God values obedience, faithfulness to the truth one knows. In Jer 35, the Rechabites are commended because they stayed faithful to the charge their ancestor gave them to never drink wine, build houses, or plant anything, but to be nomadic. The Lord uses them as an example to the people of Israel who have *not* listened to the Lord. Were the Rechabites prepared from before, for reasons they didn't know, for this moment when they would be God's flannel board? How much of what we do in faithfulness, obedience to some nudge within, is used at some later time by God?

---

1. May, *Dark Night of the Soul*, 72–73.

Yesterday, a friend told me that something I had done a year or so ago, God had used to comfort her last week. When her husband was coming to the end of his battle against brain cancer, he had a procedure involving setting a steel circlet into his skull, attached by screws, to guide the beams of the therapeutic radiation machine. I had sat with my friend in the waiting room, while he was being prepared, and we had a long, good conversation, drawing us much closer than we had been. Her husband later passed away. Last week, she had watched a program on TV showing a similar procedure, and she felt "set back" into her grief, with memories of that time with her husband flooding in. But, she said, she had a strong sense of my presence with her, as I had been on that day, which comforted her greatly. I am so deeply moved by this—how God prepared this good work beforehand, knowing what use he would make of it beyond the moment. This is grace, and a great gift to me, to hear how God used that memory to steady and comfort her amidst the other hard memories.

September 25. Jer 28: The word of God to the king: Surrender to the Babylonians. What will the king do? He is a weak king, subject to the officials. If he were strong, he might call a city-wide assembly to humble himself and the people before God, telling them what God had said, and leading them out to surrender. It would not look good, though. Kings aren't supposed to surrender to their enemies. Jeremiah assures the king that he will be treated well if he obeys God. The king knows that God speaks through Jeremiah, and he has often sought the word of God through Jeremiah. But *this* word? How important it is to obey the voice of the Lord regularly, so that when it seems peculiar, the habit will kick in, and we will obey—if *you* say so, Lord. The king is Mr. Facing-Both-Ways. As I am, often, compliant with what I think "people" expect of me, and wanting also to do God's will. Lord, give me strength to be obedient, today, to *your* voice.

September 29. God's funny at times; I got a quick cartoon from him in prayer: "Fines double in construction zones." I must go slowly through this area of inner construction—no speeding!

October 1. It occurred to me in dance class today that before I can go to Rwanda I need to find the *me* that God wants to use and minister to and through. There must be no tinge of false or egocentric sacrifice. It must be Isaac that I offer—this occurs just now; what is most precious to me, God's best gift and joy? Then I remembered Saul's arrogation to himself of the sacrifice Samuel was to make, because Saul got worried that the people were defecting, and he would lose his authority and power against the massed enemy. Samuel had told him to *wait* seven days, and he, Samuel, would come and offer the sacrifices. Now Saul has waited seven days, and no Samuel, so he assumes it must be up to him to call upon the Lord, to avoid defeat. So he "forces himself" to do this. And loses the Lord's favor as king. (1 Sam 13:8–15). I feel the Lord has given me this as both a caution and an encouragement. *Wait* for him; I am not to offer a self-centered sacrifice, but he will come and offer the right sacrifice—in his time. Even if it seems things are slipping out of my control, or people begin to wonder about this "call" I've received, I am to wait. The encouraging thing is that *when* God comes, he will have something right and true and good for me to have dominion over. Friend Kristi's prayer comes to mind: that God will give me an authority and power I have not known, and not through my understanding. Dear Lord Jesus, you are sovereign over all things and events. With your strong help, I will wait.

October 2. Mary's assent, "Let it be with me according to your word" (Luke 1:38 NRSV), is obedience to a particular calling—not just "anything you want, Lord," but yes, I will receive *this* from you. Elizabeth says this beautiful thing: "Blessed is she who believed that there would be a fulfillment of what was spoken to her by the Lord" (Luke 1:45 NRSV). By faith was the Son of Man brought into the world. Extraordinary dependence of God upon human willingness. Elizabeth is a model of encouragement—she sees what God has done in Mary's life, and what he will do, and blesses her, specifically focusing on Mary's believing heart as the crux of the matter. Lord, this is what I desire to do and be for people—encourage them.

October 20. A strong word from the Lord: "The Lord has said to you, 'You must never return that way [to Egypt] again'" (Deut 17:16 NRSV). I am called out of the world to serve and trust God. There is always a temptation to return to Egypt for more horses, or for what is known and accessible—but I am to remember God's injunction.

October 28. "But when one turns to the Lord, the veil is removed" (2 Cor 3:16 NRSV). As I turned to him just now, I sensed the veil of self-control and emotional distance lifting, and tears came. There are various kinds of veils. Turning to the Lord lifts them, because he is Truth. Reality.

November 12. God is faithful, patient, kind. I am a dork. God loves me, even so. A dear, deep time of God's visitation—tears of joy and love. My prayer was, "Thank you for coming." And I "saw" how wonderful Jesus was when he came and exposed himself to the hypocrisy of the Jewish leaders. Under the eye of religion gone bad, he boldly loved—teaching, healing, blessing—and gave himself to God and to all of us. Such a mighty man! I am flooded with amazement and awareness. . . . Now I am returned from a transport of joy and love into the ordinary day. This is where I am to live out what I have been privileged to see and feel.

December 1. God does not forsake his children, as I did mine. Nor does he condemn me, as I still condemn myself. Grace is poured out freely—and I am wearing a raincoat.

December 4. "The Lord is faithful in all his words, and gracious in all his deeds. The Lord upholds all who are falling, and raises up all who are bowed down" (Ps 145:13b–14 NRSV). A moment of sanity and clarity: I ask the Lord in quietness and trust to prepare me for whatever he has for me to do in Rwanda, and to prepare that situation for me, and to help me to wait in patience, keeping my confidence in him, not frightened by anything— just wait and trust that God will reveal things at the right time.

January 9. It seems wonderful that over the centuries, God has consistently revealed himself to people, who have testified to his greatness, love, actions—all in tune, each testimony recognizable as stamped by God's love and unchanging character. True, there are many imperfections, slubs, in the fabric of testimony, but as with raw silk, these only serve to enhance the overall beauty and organic perfection that is Christ in us, revealed in, through, and by *us.*

January 14. "The Lord will fulfill his purpose for me; your steadfast love, O Lord, endures forever. Do not forsake the work of your hands" (Ps 138:8 NRSV).

January 24. He has counseled me, given me the confirmation I asked for—to glorify and praise his name. Antoine [then team leader of AEE-Rwanda] has clearly spelled out a ministry for me among prostitutes and former prostitutes, and I have the sense that this is God's answer to my question about purpose in going.

January 29. The ebb and flow of joy and peace, insight and praise unsettles me, until I realize this movement is of God's Spirit, like the ocean's surf—the withdrawal of the wave that exposes the sand and gravel, and leaves me blinking, wobbly, and sinking in wet sand, is not the withdrawal of God's presence, only his great indrawn breath, to blow the wave back again, surely, and catch me up—maybe tumble me about or even dunk me—but always lifting me, always. The experience of flooding tears and my filled and praising heart is his gift, and as this is withdrawn for a time, I get to draw my breath deeply and wait *actively,* expectantly, in hope and quietness of soul, for his return. It is his word that anchors me in these times, as it is his word that exalts my spirit in those times of surging presence.

February 15. Humility continues to rise in my consciousness as the Lord's focus: "He leads the humble in what is right, and teaches the humble his way" (Ps 25:9 NRSV). I am to humble myself, *and* God will humble me. Then I can be taught and led, and fed from God's word.

My God! How he has worked in me just now—following reading Jer 7:21–34, he gave me a glimpse of his anguish over the perversions and horrors his people have perpetrated—such grief engulfed me—and in tears I was led to deep consecration to him, to be made pure and holy for whatever work he has for me. The armor of God is perfectly guarding me, and his great love is blessing me. No words can describe this—but I wanted to note this holy moment as a milestone of God's amazing grace.

June 17. [Daughter] PJ's last day here. How to say goodbye!? We are one in the Lord—a blessing and comfort. Visit with [daughter] Xan and her husband at their new home was brief, but good. Their gorgeous high grasses swaying under a large sky filled with white cumulus—space and wind and bowing grass. I may have one more chance to see Xan before I go. I feel the stroke of separation keenly from time to time, and then it subsides into the activities and beauties of the day. To be here at [friend] Char's home, to see the laden dogwoods framing the lake, a heron gliding in its purposeful and unhurried approach to its next landing, a hawk stretched out to receive the current of the high sky—to be in the sweet and nurturing and fun presence of Char—what gifts!

June 20. In Denver airport. On very little sleep. Aware that God has brought me through one change after another with a minimum of stress, no disaster, a smoothness that seems remarkable—his guiding hand. I'm wondering what he has for me now. A brief moment of prayer and surrender brought tears—wonder, awe, Holy Spirit?

Next stop, Kigali, Rwanda.

7

Beginnings

Only begin . . .
There's much to be said for beginning—
Do the first indicated thing,
Take the first step,
The hardest, so they say.
Begin the race, the climb.
Begin the poem,
Begin to pray.
After creation, all beginnings simply pick up
Where somebody else left off.
Where I left off, left loose ends,
Or failed somehow.
I hear:
Begin again: He will do a new thing.
Bright and holy things await my first step,
Like skis poised, ready,
I am flung gasping down the shining mountain.

JUST BEFORE LEAVING FOR Rwanda, I wrote to my friends.

I wanted to bring you up to date on how God has been leading
me in my plan to return to Rwanda to live for a while. First, I am
amazed at how much interest this is generating, and I conclude

that God's intention is to focus many minds, hearts, and prayers on the small, courageous, conflicted, and hopeful country of Rwanda. I have been operating on prayer power such that all details of getting myself and my household ready for this move are being dealt with, with the indispensable help of my care team and other friends, and I am keeping on keeping on! I have succumbed to chocolate only occasionally!

The plan at this point is that I will be sent by my church, First Presbyterian, Bellevue, Washington, as a missionary to come under the wing of African Evangelistic Enterprise (AEE), the Rwandan branch of African Enterprise (AE), which is a partner of our church. I will leave on July 11, arriving in the capital city of Kigali on July 12, and am invited to stay either with Antoine Rutayasire (AEE team leader in Rwanda) and his family, or at the AEE guest house until a more permanent lodging can be arranged. Meanwhile, I will be working on learning the language (Kinyarwanda) and getting to know the people I will be working with. My ministry will focus on the women whom AEE is helping to give up prostitution and trust Jesus for their livelihood. Most of these women have been infected with HIV, and have AIDS; many have children, most have nothing, and all have suffered one way or another in the genocide of 1994, or in earlier times of violence. And, amazingly, many are filled with the joy that only Jesus can give. I also have been asked to help with some photography and reporting work for AEE.

I flew to Rwanda. I took only two bags, having a sense that I was to start and stay light, in terms of material things. Though I had been well-sent, I was now on my own, trusting to God and the folks at AEE to gather me up and set me on my feet in the hot, smoky, populous, and colorful city of Kigali, the capital.

For the first few months in Kigali, I stayed at the AEE guest house, where I was able to begin connecting with people from AEE (administrative and kitchen staff), and also with people who wanted to visit me from outside the compound. I stayed in one of the suites, which had a central sitting room. That became my de facto living room, where I had my first language lessons, ate my meals, and began to feel my way with people whose language and culture was so different than mine. Though I was quite alone, I was guided very graciously and sacrificially into the intricacies of my new city and country by members of the senior staff of AEE and others. John Kalenzi, then second in command to the team leader Antoine, took me under his wing, and became a sort of tour guide. He showed me Kigali—on one occasion boarding a local and very crowded bus with me so I could learn how the transportation system worked—and took me out of the city when he had business elsewhere, using those visits to show me memorial sites or other places of interest.

Language lessons

My main focus in those early months was to learn Kinyarwanda. I had already begun while still in the states to use my Kinyarwanda Bible to help me pick out words, but now I engaged a language helper, and threw myself into daily study and practice. I used a method of study I had learned through the PILAT (Program in Language Acquisition Techniques) system when I attended a course in Colorado Springs, just before coming to Rwanda. That system emphasizes frequent practice in a variety of settings of whatever is being studied. After a short period of fearfulness, I ventured out onto the road near AEE where there were small shops and a market, and where there were always people: on bicycles, on foot, carrying a variety of things on their heads, and always staring at me, or calling out, "*muzungu, muzungu!*" (white person). I learned to counteract their dull stares with a smile and a greeting, and was always rewarded by faces lighting up with pleasure. It seemed that many people kept their face expressionless, perhaps as a way of defending themselves by not letting anyone know what's going on inside them. (Over the years, as I learned more about the Rwandese people and their experiences, I developed a better understanding about this protectiveness, and its causes.) But they always enjoyed interacting with me, which encouraged me. I would try the little Kinyarwanda I knew, usually failing utterly to understand the responses, but always eliciting delighted laughter whenever anyone heard me attempt to speak their language.

I once had a hilarious exchange of misunderstandings: while buying a pineapple in a small nearby market, I asked the price. I was told "magana ane," which means four hundred francs—a very reasonable price! But in my nascent ability with the number system, what I *heard* was "magana inani," eight hundred francs, which I thought rather exorbitant. (Perhaps you can see that the words look very similar; my ear was not yet attuned to hearing the crucial difference between four hundred and eight hundred francs.) So, I decided to try to bargain with the lady—I offered *six* hundred francs (which, of course, was two hundred francs *above* the price she had quoted). She laughed (it seemed to me in scorn that I should try to bring the price down so much), and said, no, it's four hundred (and I again heard eight hundred). In the end, I never understood my error, and she ended up with two hundred francs more than she had asked for—a very satisfactory, if puzzling, outcome for her. For me, I came away in the glow of having successfully bargained the price down from eight hundred to six hundred francs. It was sometime later, as I reviewed this transaction in my mind, that it occurred to me what had actually happened. I had to laugh!

While working on the language—using the words and phrases I learned as much as possible—I developed relationships with a few people, and began the long journey of discovery and discernment about what God was up to in bringing me there. I continued in daily prayer, Bible reading and journal writing, knowing that my strength and wisdom must come from my relationship with God and from knowing his word as it could apply to each day's questions and challenges. I had rather a lot of ideas, each seeming to be significant and useful, about how I might spend my time. My biggest trial, perhaps, was to know how to respond to certain people's hopes and expectations. In a journal entry from July 19, 2005, I recorded a conversation with Antoine, who was then team leader for AEE, and my mentor: "Antoine enjoined me with many words not to be taken in by anyone requesting my help ("prayers," etc.)—that Rwandese are *not* direct—but I can just tell them I am here as a missionary, on support from others, and will be praying for God's leading about what I am to do. He says, never promise anyone anything—if I want to help someone, OK to do so, but work it out in my own heart."

Looking back, I am most grateful for that advice, and I wish others coming to developing countries would also hear such wise words. Promises are easily inferred when a white person says, "I'll think about it," or, "let me know how things go." I suffered much over the years, from the results of having apparently promised something I had no power to follow up on. In these early days, there were two people who were quite sure that God had directed me to them to be the channel for his resources to make their vision a reality. Because I longed to be of service, and was very uncertain of how this would come about, and because these two had become my friends in 2004 when I came the first time, it seemed right and good that I continue developing our relationships. But gradually I found I was being drawn into a demand for a level of involvement I could not possibly fulfill. Fortunately, I did *not* promise them anything, but my very interest and concern for their visions, my willingness to meet with them and pray with them, constituted in their minds a commitment on my part. I found it difficult, and necessary, to extricate myself from this complex entanglement, but somehow was able to do so without losing them as friends. With one, I continued to stay open to ways I could be available as a Bible teacher, which he valued. With the other, I tried to stay friends on a personal level, and when she married and began to have a family, to be an encouragement to her. But for her, her ministry vision always came first, and since I had reservations about it (which I shared with her), our friendship could only go so far.

My Rwandan friends were beginning to tell me what they saw in my future here—what they believed God would do in me. One woman told me I was to be an intercessor and a spiritual help to the people here (which I could agree would be a good thing!); another told me that I would be used mightily by God, and that when I preached, God would give me power to bless people, and which words to say. I'd better pray a lot, she said—and she was praying daily for me. As for me, I was still wondering and seeking for my purpose. After all, I had only just arrived in Rwanda!

Unique in Christ

On July 17, I wrote in my journal,

> Lord, I suddenly realize I don't want to waste my time here—I don't know how long I'll be here. My life is not my own. I'm not here to be catered to, loved—but to do what you have prepared for me to do. This means prayer, letting go of comforts, willingness to seek you, so that you will reveal your purpose for me. Three times I have been told that you have planned something big for me to do. Lord, if you have spoken to these people about me, would you begin to show me what you have in mind? How shall I prepare to hear your voice? Humble myself, I hear. Wait for the Lord.

Then on July 20, I rediscovered—as though for the first time—what has become a main theme of my life since this journey began. "A light shone on the extraordinary fact that I am a unique channel of God's love—no one else can shape God's love the way I can, if I am emptied of self and cleansed and clear for him. This brings joy, not arrogance—I don't channel God's love better than anyone else—just uniquely—as each person does."

While in this process of learning, exploring, waiting, discovering, I helped out at AEE with some writing tasks, including a couple of concept notes for proposed projects. One was for an extension of the healing and reconciliation work AEE was doing into school curricula and parent education, which focused on trauma counseling so kids wouldn't perpetuate the unresolved anger of parents. It was sent off just as I wrote it, and received a positive response from the donor. It felt good to be useful, but I wondered if this was what I was here to do.

In my first letter to friends from Kigali on July 20, 2005, I wrote,

> I want to give God praise for so many blessings: an exceedingly soft landing, providing me with safe travel, perfect connections, lovely travel-mates, and most gratefully, Antoine at the airport. (I only saw him *after* I had negotiated the visa line (no charge for US citizens, so just an easy stamp and a welcome), the baggage (the power went off and on, so it came limpingly along the belt), wrestling both seventy pound bags onto a cart without even slightly injuring myself (!), and trundling them through customs line with no hitch. All the way, there were little flutters of anxiety—what ifs—but God was so gracious to smooth it all before me.
>
> So far, I have been to Rwamagana, about an hour drive from here, where AEE is training street kids in various skills—a modest but well-conceived program, it seems to me. Also got to visit Green Pastures, for helping prostitutes, and hope to return to learn more.
>
> Today, I latched onto Philippians 1: 9–11, which I have begun to memorize, and hope to make a regular, daily prayer: "And this is my prayer, that your love may overflow more and more with knowledge and full insight to help you to determine what is best, so that in the day of Christ you may be pure and blameless, having produced the harvest of righteousness that comes through Jesus Christ for the glory and praise of God." I pray this for you, too.

As I prayed for guidance, or in intercession, or in praise, tears frequently came—as they still do—and I considered them a confirmation of the Holy Spirit that I was praying within his purpose, and touching his heart. I wanted God to deepen this prayer life in me. Along the way, I felt he revealed himself and his desire for me beautifully. Here, for example, on July 28:

> Saw a lovely thing: As I try to offer God something—myself, all that I am and have—I see that I can offer him only what he has given me, all is his—but he *has* given me the wherewithal to offer him something. It's like the child who wants to buy her mother a gift, so she asks her mother for money, not telling her what it's for. But the mother knows, understands, and gives the child the money so she can go buy a gift to bring with great joy to her mother. God is blessed by my offering to him what he has given

45

me—like Hannah offering Samuel. Each day, each moment, I can offer him something because he has so richly blessed me. *And,* the more I offer, the more blessings I receive, and his blessings are for many more than me.

8

What to Do?

IN THE MONTHS AFTER arriving in Rwanda, I was in a state of deep pondering, active experimentation, and rather disorganized ministry activities, as I tried to figure out what I was there for. Sometimes I was pressed into service, so far with no office of my own, for urgent work that wasn't much fun. Even in this, I could sense God reaching out to teach me. From my current vantage point, as I look back over the process I went through to discover what I was to do in Rwanda, I find it fascinating to see how many ideas I either was given or that came to me in the first few months about what my work should be.

In a conversation with Antoine, who confirmed my idea that I needed to study and take my time about deciding where I would serve, he proposed a possible renewing of a defunct "Ruth/Naomi club," which consisted of former prostitutes reaching out to street girls. I knew I would have to really know Kinyarwanda well in order to do any such ministry.

Or, I would work with Green Pastures, a project run by a Rwandese woman named Annie, who started good work with prostitutes, giving them a home and seeking to retrain them from the mind-set of the street to learning to trust God, while also being trained in various skills—crafts, sewing, etc. This idea came out of a chance conversation one evening with AEE's Charles, who had stopped to greet me. I asked him to tell me about that ministry which I knew he oversaw. Here is the journal entry for July 30:

> As we talked, my interest grew, and I could sense a tug within, encouraging me to proceed with this connection. I told Charles I'd

like to begin coming along, to spend some time with the women, building trust, listening, praying, and seeking to show God's love and compassion to them. Charles felt that this had been God's appointment, and that he should immediately take me up on this. I think God has done some work in my heart since I first arrived, and I feel I may be ready to begin learning about this ministry and how I might help. I praise him!

Internal pressure about my purpose in Rwanda was increasing; another entry:

Asking God to show me my path in his kingdom. I feel strong upwelling of need to know. Don't know if that's him moving in me, or my own need. I find I want to make a home somewhere, to nest, and to have a place to invite others. [At this time, I was reading the story of the Israelites' journey in the wilderness on their way to the Promised Land. That story has often been helpful, instructive, encouraging, and cautionary for my own journey. In response to reading in Deut 1, I wrote:] It is the Lord who goes before you, Moses told them, "to seek out a place for you to camp . . . to show you the route you should take" (verse 33). Well, that seems directed to my plea! I should review what God has done so far in leading me, and taking care of every need. He called me, invited me, sent me here with his mighty power overcoming all obstacles—and there was not even any opposition. He cleared the way before me, giving me ideas, a strong and committed and loving team, many, many loving, prayerful farewells, money unlooked-for, equipment—computer, camera—safe travel, good health, and a heart that finds its home here. He has stirred up a spirit of prayer, given me discernment, wisdom, love for specific people—indeed he has carried me "just as one carries a child, all the way that you traveled until you reached this place" (verse 31). Remember that God has sent me here. So, what route should I take? God wants me to trust him, always, and to remember his faithfulness. He has shown me where to camp, and where the next day's route goes. One day at a time. He's given me the very large picture—go to Rwanda—and the very small details of each day's journey. What do I need besides?

Prayer and seeking God continued. August 17, I wrote: "I felt so thankful, again, that God brought me here—as though there had been a hole shaped like me, which only I could fill. Truly I have never felt so in the *right* place.

A special bond

Some kind of involvement with Solace Ministries was also being discussed. Started after the genocide by Jean Gakwandi, a survivor with all his family, Solace ministers primarily to widows and other women survivors, most living with AIDS. When I was in Rwanda the first time in 2004, God arranged a number of special connections with various people during that period, and one of those instant bonds was made between me and Jean. Our team had visited Solace as part of the planned events we were participating in with AEE, and I had been quite interested in the work and spirit of that ministry. But it wasn't until the culmination of the commemoration of the tenth anniversary of the genocide that the bond was formed between me and Jean.

It happened like this: The final event was a march from a roundabout in Kigali to the main stadium called Amahoro ("peace"). It was a very hot day—we were in the midst of the dry season—and I was not able to keep up with the marchers in my team. I didn't worry about getting lost, as I would just follow the crowd, but that crowd got thinner and thinner as I fell behind. As I walked, a young woman came alongside and began to talk to me, asking where I was going. I told her, and said I had got separated from my group, and wondered if she was also going to the stadium. She was a student, she said, and was going near there, and would be glad to accompany me. And so she did, taking my hand in the lovely way many people do in Rwanda. Arrived at the stadium, we parted—having exchanged contact information—and I was left to find my way into the huge stadium. I had no idea which of the several entrances to try, and I was by this time very hot and somewhat weak. I prayed a bit, trusting God to help me. As I climbed some stairs leading into the stadium, and came out where I could look around at the people, I saw no sign of any white face; my team seemed to have been swallowed up in the sea of Rwandese people.

I started back down the stairs, at a loss about what to do, when a man called me by name, and asked what I was doing there. I told him I was lost, and how did he know my name? He said he had seen me at Solace, and knew where my team was seated. He almost literally gathered me up, and took me around to the right entrance and up the stairs to where my team was seated. That was Jean Gakwandi. Not only did he reconnect me with my team, but he sat with me for the ceremonies. During that brief time, we somehow became very close, though it is strange and difficult to explain how such an intimacy could have sprung up so quickly. He told me many things about his life as a genocide survivor, and about his work at

Solace. He promised to send me a Kinyarwanda Bible in the states after I returned—and he did.

So when I was planning to come back to Rwanda, one possibility of where to work and stay was Solace, Jean's ministry. For various reasons that didn't happen, but I remained in touch, and we continued to hug each other warmly whenever we met. I did, however, visit Jean on my return, and we discussed some way I could be ministering to the genocide survivors (mostly women living with AIDS) who met once a week at Solace. Before long, we decided I would come to that weekly meeting, hoping for God's leading as to how I could encourage or counsel the women who were in such need of both.

Share the story

Although I had no experience preaching, I found in these early ministry experiences that the most important thing I could do was to share the story of my sinful life and God's redemption, connecting my testimony to words in the Bible that I discerned might be an encouragement to the listeners. It seemed that God often used these times to move people toward a deeper connection with him.

In addition to the weekly Solace meetings, I began to have a stronger pull toward Green Pastures, and I began to visit them twice a week. I struggled to communicate with Annie, whose passion bordered on obsession, and who seemed to be unwilling to listen to or receive my input. With Charles' help, we were trying to get her to put a board together and to become more organized and less impulsive in the way she did ministry. On one occasion when I visited, she had just collected some new girls to come to the house, who had been nearly naked on the streets the night before, and she urged me to preach the gospel to them. After doing the best I could, and having learned their names, I prayed for those who wished to have prayer, several of whom wanted to start (or start again) with Jesus as their Lord.

Meanwhile, Joseph Nyamutera of Le Rucher Mercy Ministries, who was then at AEE, also frequently involved me in some of the work in healing and reconciliation he was doing, which I loved being a part of. When he began to envision his retreat/debriefing center, he told me he thought I could be helpful in that work. He invited me to join him on a three-day mission to pastors to be held in Gitarama, about two hours south of Kigali. In the car on the way there, Joseph told me I was to give devotions each morning. I was learning that in Rwanda, if you are known to be a "servant of God," you will be asked to preach, everyone assuming that you have something worthwhile to say—and also, that you don't need any advance warning or time to prepare!

That retreat turned out to be a great opportunity for me, showing me both how God is ready to meet me and use me with little preparation on my part, and also how he wants to grow me in awareness of others' needs—especially in this culture. As I rode toward Gitarama with this sudden assignment ringing in my ears, I asked God what on earth I should do, *could* do, in these three successive morning devotions. His answer came swiftly: use the story of Gideon. Perhaps my readers are familiar with the man to whom God sent an angel while he was cowering in the wine press out of fear of the Israelites' enemy number one of the day, the Midianites. He was addressed as "mighty warrior," which of course he felt didn't fit him at all. The story tells of how God gave him confidence to completely defeat the powerful oppressors, using a paltry three-hundred-man force and some pottery. Somehow, I felt God leading me to use this story as a way to encourage the pastors at this conference.

I don't recall what I taught, but I will recount the main teaching I *received* from this experience. After the first session, which I felt had gone amazingly well—I had given a lot of great content and it all flowed beautifully—I asked Joseph for feedback. "Well," he said, "it would have been good if you had told them something about yourself." He wanted me to see that what I taught was not nearly as important as sharing who I was. After all, these pastors had never seen me before, and knew nothing of my journey with Christ. Chastened and humbled, I started the second session with my story, working back into the story of Gideon in the process. That seemed to make a crucial difference, and I have never forgotten that lesson.

Antoine had originally thought I might come to live with his family for a time, but as time went on, and my various activities were developing, he told me he felt moving away from AEE at this time would disrupt my ministry, which he pronounced "wonderful"—which amazed me, as it seemed such a hodgepodge to me, and also because Antoine does not give compliments lightly or easily. I remained for a time at the guesthouse.

> *September 16, 2005.* Each day is full of new experiences, challenges, and joys. Antoine and I have decided I won't move in with his family, since I am well launched in ministry and pretty well started in language study. He kindly offered his home as a retreat,

where I could come to "my room" for a night or two and just hang out with his family and play with the cat (which Antoine pronounces "kot"). So I am now looking for a home of my own. I am also working on getting a driver's permit and establishing resident status. Meanwhile, I use AEE drivers—a blessing, as I've become friends with them all, but I'm dependent on their availability. I need to depend on feet and public transport more! It looks like I will become a staff member of AEE (details to be worked out). I feel committed to this organization, and want to focus within it as God leads me.

We have had some rain—so refreshing, and lovely to see green and flowers come quickly after only a little rain. Language study continues, now with a formal teacher named Issa, recommended by a new missionary friend named Kristi, who speaks fluent Kinyarwanda with Issa's help, so I'm hopeful! I use what I can remember whenever I get the chance, making "conversation" such as: Me (in Kinyarwanda): How is your wife? Placide: She is sick. (Then I'm stuck for a response, and have to lapse into French; it turns out she may have an amoebic disorder.) With Yolande, my friend in the kitchen, I've been relying on French, but she wants to learn English. So we've made a pact: I speak only Kinyarwanda with her, and she responds only in English.

I'm amazingly well! God is so *good* to keep me healthy. I've tumbled twice, which is scary, but no serious damage done. Kristi has included me in a missionaries Bible study on Sunday afternoon; I have begun a prayer partnership, and I believe I've found my church home—a Presbyterian church just down the road, which several AEE staff go to. It seemed very right and good to me; excellent sermon on Jonah (a new friend interpreting), lots of good music and joy, and yet a kind of "everything decently and in order" feel about it. Communion for the first time since I came—most refreshing!

In ministry, I have felt God working to humble me in new ways, reminding me that none of this work is to focus on me, but on God. I can subtly think more highly of myself than I ought to think, especially as I'm sort of a celebrity just by virtue of being white and making my home here.

A hand up

As my circle of friends grew, I began looking at how to help meet some of the many needs I learned about. Gilbert, who later became like a son to me, began to talk about his goals. The first time we met to discuss his future, he knew no English and I knew only a little Kinyarwanda, so we had Jerome interpret. I had asked him to think about a plan for a business or project I might be able to either help with or advise about. That first meeting he presented me with a very big idea—involving hundreds of dollars. I suggested that he might want to focus on something more immediately manageable, and he went to have another go at it.

Eventually, he came up with a workable plan. He would buy local crafts and make them available for sale at the AEE guest house. A friend and I funded the start of that business, which involved getting in a small variety of craft items and a display shelf, and he took off with it. It happened to be a time in AEE's history when there were many guests coming and going, and they appreciated the convenience of being able to buy carefully selected crafts practically at their doorstep. As a result of this small project, Gilbert was able to expand to provide other services to visitors, and soon saved enough money to be able to marry Esther, his long-time sweetheart. Along the way, he also accomplished two other goals: he learned English and he got his driving license. He has since graduated from university and completed a master's degree, having found excellent jobs that have increased his range of experience and skills. He was able to achieve these goals primarily because he is a man of prayer and much diligence.

This experience with Gilbert was the first round in what turned out to be a major theme and role in my life in Rwanda. I realized very early on that entrepreneurship could play a crucial role in getting people up and out of poverty and the hand-out mentality. As I discussed ideas with Gilbert, I was thinking of ways to help him, and others, develop a business mind-set. This seems extraordinary, looking back, as I'd had zero interest in or experience with business prior to coming to Rwanda. But it developed into a major portion of my thinking, prayer, and work.

How (not) to rent a house

While searching for my work and ministry focus, the practical matter of finding a place to live on my own, away from the AEE guest house, was proving to be challenging. In Rwanda one doesn't have access to the classified section of the newspaper to find rental homes or apartments. You have to either know someone who knows how to find places for rent, or hire a professional "commissioner" to help you, or just put the word out that you're looking for a place. I decided to hire a commissioner, and after a bit of looking, I found a place—but the experience was most distressing. I got the coldest feet on record, after having given the landlord two months' rent. I just *knew* I couldn't live in that dark, damp house. What had possessed me? The landlord sounded extremely puzzled over the phone when I told him I wanted to un-rent his house. I never did get that money back. So I remained at AEE for a time, until God opened up the way to the house that was right for me.

After licking my wounds for a few weeks following the house debacle, I was still staying at the AEE guest house. One day, a woman at church told me Antoine had mentioned my need of a house to rent, and she invited me to look at one she was hoping to rent out. Over the years, I've found that if I listen, the house I'm meant to live in will speak to me. Hers did. It was a quirky sort of place—shaped like a three-fold version of a thatched hut, but made of bricks and tile, set on a large plot full of tall trees and flowers. It was the place for me, and became my home for the next five years.

Deeper into ministry

As my work developed, I kept expanding my range. I got to know and connect with several leaders and groups. My focus was with street people—prostitutes and other youth and children. Youth With a Mission (YWAM) had a base down the road, and a wonderful young leader (called Serieux) had collected a group of women of the streets to hear the gospel and pray together once a week. I was invited to meet with them. How distressed, despairing, darkened, dirty, deranged, and damaged those women appeared to me! But God is able to give hope, light, cleanliness, sanity, and healing, and I trusted he would show us the way. I also went with a committed street pastor called Theoneste to one of his street kids meetings. There, the children and youths were clean, radiated joy, and basking in the love Theoneste and his volunteers communicated from God. Although they were changing by God's grace, they still had nowhere to go, nothing to do. None of them were in school, and few could read or write. I think God was showing me that beyond the gospel, we should begin teaching these people to read and write.

Another time I went with Theoneste to preach in the rain to a different group of boys sitting on the muddy hillside under a mango tree in the area where they lived—no shelter, hardly any clothing, who knows how they survived—and felt grieved and frustrated by their plight. What could we do? What could the churches do? What would they be willing to do? Theoneste asked me to follow up on my preaching (about David and Goliath) by leading the boys to Christ. I did, awkwardly, and prayed for them all, huddled together in a group. The boys gave their lives to Jesus, but I was disturbed about this kind of quick-conversion approach, because I didn't think they had a clue about who Jesus is or what it means to be saved. If I only had one chance at them, I figured I'd better prepare a teaching about Jesus! Both Serieux and Theoneste were men whom I was soon to invite into the network I formed in 2006.

Visa adventure

My visa was about to expire, and since the required documentation was not ready for getting the missionary visa I needed, I was whisked off to cross the border into Tanzania, hopefully to get my passport stamped for an automatic ninety-day renewal, and return. Didn't work! The border guard was unimpressed with my story that I just wanted to hop over the bridge to "see Tanzania"; he knew my only interest in Tanzania was to get my passport stamped with another visa. In the process, having urgently needed a restroom, I rammed a nail into my finger as I closed the filthy restroom door at a nearby restaurant, and had to be taken to a local clinic—terrified about the level of care I might receive. As it turned out, I had one suture put in with skill and good attention to sterility, and returned to AEE somewhat the worse for wear, though without a renewed visa. Nevertheless, I had a grand time riding home in the dark with driver Theogene preaching in Kinyarwanda about how God will take care of my visa, since he made everything there is! (He did, with AEE's help.)

Every month AEE has a prayer and fasting day, which includes a focus on the word, and from time to time I was asked to prepare something to present. On one of the first of such occasions, I preached on the fearful mind-set, and how it robs God's people of their blessing, making them useless for his work (many illustrations of this, unfortunately, in the Bible!). I counteracted this with the love-oriented mind-set (perfect love casts out fear). God blessed this time, and used it to bring some deep fears to light in two of the young women, whom we prayed for. One of these had been enslaved for years by a fear of marriage. As we prayed, she was totally set free from that fear. It was a touching movement of the Holy Spirit.

Trusted to choose

Now my prayers began to take a turn: I began to wonder if I should actually make a choice about what I wanted to do, myself, without having some sort of direct and specific word from God. I knew, from previous experience with the Holy Spirit, that he often does invite me into this sort of partnership with him, encouraging me to make a choice, and to trust him in my choosing.

In my journal for September 16, I wrote,

> Is it the same now? Lord, it seems too much freedom! I know, "for freedom Christ has set us free," but in this thing, Lord? I'm led to think about Paul in his decisions. In Acts 13, the "prophets and teachers"—including Barnabas and Saul—were worshiping and fasting. Then the Holy Spirit spoke to them to set apart Barnabas and Saul "for the work to which I have called them." They continued fasting and praying, then laid hands on the two men and "sent them off." And then, "being sent out by the Holy Spirit, they went . . . to Cyprus" and began preaching to the Jews. (Barnabas' role in Saul's life is what I want to be in people's lives here.)

As I followed Paul and Barnabas in their journeys, seeking to understand the ways God led them, I saw that Paul had overall a primary focus: to preach the gospel. Within that focus, he was led in various ways, including directly by the Holy Spirit, but also by the circumstances and responses he received. On several occasions I noticed also that Paul made his own plans and carried them out (unless blocked by the spirit of God). I asked God for this kind of freedom: to both know my overall purpose, and the freedom to move within it. I was so encouraged by my study of how God is faithful to lead his servants in the story of the early church in Acts. Bottom line: God leads his people! I wrote, "Paul *uses* his mind, his training, his experience, his keen observation, to make the most of every opportunity to persuade people to follow Christ. Within the calling, God wants us to strive mightily."

Also, as I studied through the book of Acts, I saw how Paul repeatedly gave his testimony, shaping it differently each time for his audience, but always with the intent of persuading his hearers to follow Christ. I had already realized through my experience in teaching the pastors that I also was to use my testimony. And in fact, that is what I did; each time I had an opportunity to preach or teach in a new place where I was not known, I found a way to include the testimony of how God brought me out of a life of sin into a life of freedom to serve him. I don't know how many people may have been touched in some way by this testimony—God knows—but I have been faithful to tell my story.

A heart of love in this culture

By now, mid-September of my first year, though I was fairly clear that I was somehow to be involved in ministry to prostitutes, I was concerned about the state of my heart toward these women. Journal entry of September 23:

> One big thing is needed: a *heart* for this work. Can I say that I have it now? What would that be like? I would pray hard for them. I would have compassion for them. I would not despise them or seek to distance myself from them. I would extend myself for them, sacrifice for them. I am not fully there—but I believe God will give me a heart as I go forward.
>
> In my search for ministry and focus, I continued to understand that the "wilderness" was important, instructive at this time. It is only in the wilderness—deprivation of path, provision, and presence—that God can be met and known and fully worshiped. Call me out of Egypt. Let me know that you are what I am thirsty for. I am afraid of this way, but it's the only way to life. If I am going to be able to point others to Jesus in their wilderness, I have to know him in mine, as John the Baptist, Elijah, Moses, and Jesus did. Let me not be afraid, let not my enemies triumph over me. Remember all the way the Lord has led me.

As I struggled along, I can see now that God was working to develop my cultural awareness. I had to learn that Rwandese people do not act, respond, or think like I, or most Westerners, do. Without a strong and growing awareness of some of these differences, I would be ineffective and likely harmful in attempts at ministry.

> *September 28.* This situation drives me to the Lord, and to using my wits and contacts. Pondering Jesus' words in Matt 6:21: "For where your treasure is, there your heart will be also." I guess I treasure *answers*, and am troubled by uncertainty. I treasure *mobility*, independence, and am frustrated by my sense of being trapped. This drives me to determine to use public transport—which is good. I treasure comfort and nice things around me, and am distressed that I have to now spend money on things like those I already own, in storage in the states. *But,* I gave those things up to come here. Can I release the anxiety over money? I treasure *order*—clear focus

and direction. I treasure *control*—being in control, myself. This is probably the core issue now: Who is in control? Will I trust God? Father, you know everything that I need to be fruitful and happy in your kingdom. Your kingdom comes first—my emotional state is not primary. The strongholds of self must come down, and God is mighty to pull them down, to be replaced by his kingdom in me. The authority, the royal rule of the Lord, is to be established within me, displacing all other kinds of spurious control or authority.

Through all of this confusing activity—both external and within— God was continually showing me the great need I had for discipline and trust. As I reviewed that first year, I could see that God was doing a major plowing job, ready to plant some good new seeds, but a great deal of clearing had to be done first. I was clear that I was supposed to be in Rwanda— that was my anchor. But I was repeatedly unclear about God's faithfulness to show me my purpose or work, and spent my days plunging after one demand or request or need after another. I did a lot of biblical teaching (at AEE's request—to their staff at devotions and retreats, and at the sites I visited). I studied the Bible daily, pondering the passages I read to find personal application as well as direction for teaching. It seems that what God was doing was to show me both the general field in which he wanted me to be involved (street kids and prostitutes), and the dreadful state of my spiritual health. All this in the context of a culture in which I kept getting tangled up, realizing I didn't understand much about it. I was frequently frustrated and offended (not to speak of how I must have caused offense!), and often felt isolated and marginalized. The biblical theme throughout: Wait for the Lord! Rest in Him! And learn personal discipline! There is nothing like being in a strange land to discover all one's flaws and serious character defects.

But, on the other hand, God was leading me. He was also using me, sustaining (and restraining) me, repeatedly refreshing me, and teaching me richly through regular (desperate!) probing into his word. I can't imagine how the folks at AEE were able to put up with me; they not only did so, but loved me and taught me much about trusting God by the way they lived their lives.

9

Better Together

ALTHOUGH I COULDN'T KNOW it at the time, my mission mentor in the
United States, Claudia, seemed to be on a direct line to God about what was
to become my ministry before I ever left the states. From my journal of June
12, 2005 (one month before departure):

> Claudia and I caught a new glimpse of what may be part of God's
> purpose in sending me to Rwanda. There are many mini-ministry
> efforts there—I know of at least three; it may be that God wants to
> draw them together for synergism, and most, to demonstrate the
> unity we have in Christ. Rwanda is so fragmented that it would be
> wonderful if I could have some part as catalyst for models of unity
> among small efforts. . . . Would the Lord use me as I grow in rela-
> tionship with each of these to help them to talk and listen to one
> another? How they could each contribute and yet keep their own
> vision—only see it expanded beyond their imagining? My team
> says just wait for the Lord—let his plan unfold.

This notion was actually a germ of the ministry that eventually developed, but not before a lot of twists and turns along the way, some of
which I've described. In the first months of 2006, I was meeting regularly
with several small ministries around Kigali. These included Theoneste's
Muhumurize (where I had preached to the boys under the mango trees
about David and Goliath); Green Pastures (before it fell apart), led by Annie; and Imbaraga, a small ministry within a larger work with prostitutes,
whose leaders I had met. After visiting their ministry, I was impressed with
their commitment, creativity, and passion to help street kids and prostitutes

through preaching the gospel, sports, and drama. There was another ministry started from Youth With a Mission, named Twitaneho—"let us care for each other." There was Dennis, with Hand to Heart Ministry, within the framework of his church, Abundant Life. Whenever asked, I went to all of these ministries to preach or be available for counseling, or to assist with some project, or simply attend. I felt that all were dedicated and clear about their goals—to help the at-risk women and children in their purview. In April, I wrote about a visit to Twitaneho.

> Yesterday I went to visit the women of Twitaneho, and found a mother with a child, one month old, with a completely cleft lip and probably cleft palate. I promised to get help for him; he must have surgery or he will die. My heart just turned over when I saw him, and I knew I had to do something. His name is Sengiyumva—apparently a common name—meaning something like "God hears my prayer." His mom's name is Denise. Two more women are about to give birth, and one has six children. They know how not to have children, but they don't really want to prevent getting pregnant. They *love* having babies! It may be the only thing that keeps them from despair. They also need HIV/AIDS testing. Lord, such a great lot of need and pain and misery—and yet, they are eager to learn. They *are* learning to read and write and count. I gave New Testaments to four yesterday, with a promise to give one to each woman who can learn to read well enough.

The seed sprouts

It occurred to me at some point that these leaders might know each other—Kigali is a small city, and they were all working in the same field of ministry. When I began to ask some of them if they knew others of my acquaintance, no one knew about any of the others! So the idea for a network was born. Completely forgetting that Claudia and I had discussed this a year previously, I now thought it would be good if they did know each other, and that perhaps as leaders they'd like coming together to meet on a regular basis to share their experience, frustrations, prayer needs, successes, and lessons learned, and to encourage one another through prayer and visiting each other's ministries. As I began to suggest this to each one, they showed much interest in the idea. I decided to act: I arranged with AEE for a room to meet, and I invited them all to come. Here is how I reported briefly on that first meeting to my friends and prayer partners:

I want to tell you about the last few days, which may help you to see why I am rejoicing and confident in God. On Friday, I had a meeting with several leaders of various street children ministries in Kigali. I had developed a desire to have them meet with each other, in a network of support, synergism, and prayer. This first meeting was a great success. I asked them each to share about themselves, their calling to this work, and the nature of their particular ministry. As they shared, I encouraged them to ask questions of each other. In the course of two hours, they were bonded in an amazing way. They decided they wanted to meet again in two weeks, and thereafter on a regular basis, as they could see the benefits of such a network. I didn't have to sell them—they grasped it easily. This means, I believe, that the street children will be helped in significant ways, and the larger picture of their problems and some lasting solutions can emerge. The best thing is that I believe I could be taken out of the picture if necessary (I could die or something!) and they would continue and grow strong.

Isn't it peculiar and wonderful that God had already planted this very plan in my mind and heart, and that I had forgotten it until the time was ripe and right to bring it into being? If I had started out upon my arrival to try to accomplish this joining together of ministries, I doubt it would have worked well, if at all. I needed first to get my cultural feet wet, develop relationships and a heart for the work. God knew how to prepare me and the ministry for the *kairos* moment to begin. On May 5, I recorded what happened at the third meeting.

Yesterday I had the third network meeting and again felt God taking hold, giving me ideas and freedom and joy to lead the group, who are all eager to work together. I thought of an exercise to illustrate the idea of "network," asking the group to stand up, draw close together, and take someone's hand with one hand and someone else's hand with the other—not someone adjacent—with the result that we were a sort of tangle, but connected and strong. God be praised!

The members liked this symbolic linking, and from time to time over the years someone would suggest that we do it again, which seemed to put new energy and motivation into their hearts.

Focus on God's word

From the beginning, I placed a regular and strong emphasis on our need to start from and stay based on the word of God. Either I or a member would take a passage at the beginning of the meetings and spend a few minutes speaking about it, and how it might help us in our work together and with the members' beneficiaries (women and children at risk). As with much of the teaching and preaching I did in Rwanda, I drew from my devotions. Often I felt God showing me something particular from his word that I wanted to share with the network, or others.

> *May 18.* What joy and wonder has come upon me as I think of the truth in 1 John 5:4. "This is the victory that has overcome the world, even our faith." The one who overcomes the world, conquers the world, is anyone who believes that Jesus is the Son of God. Our faith conquers. There is no obstacle to our faith, because it is anchored in Jesus, the Son of God, who has himself conquered the world. No wonder Jesus was frustrated by his disciples' little faith. He could do *anything* for them, in them, through them—*if they believed.* John's whole gospel was written "so that you may believe." Nothing is more crucial. Never look at myself—my incapacities and failings, which are practically endless. Never look at the roughness and apparent impassability of the road. The thing to do is look to Jesus—author and perfecter of our *faith*—and let him do what he alone can do. *Pioneer Jesus.* I have asked my God to grant me to preach this word in power to network members, so they may be renewed and ignited with this amazing truth. By the Spirit of the Lord, may it be. *We* have nothing in ourselves, no resources—i.e., money—to do what we think God wants us to do for the children and women. We are thrown upon God. But we *have* faith. Faith is no little, wistful, insubstantial thing. Faith is the *victory*—the one thing that can overpower the opposition. Satan does everything he can to minimize or undermine our faith. And our faith, even, doesn't depend on us, but it is God's gift to us. Somehow we have been greatly privileged with faith.

From this auspicious beginning, the network had a long, if quite uneven, development. As time went on, I became quite uncertain as to whether it would succeed. In fact, I tried to kill it three different times over its history.

Problems and issues

We started our work together in March 2006. As early as June, I wrote,

> Meister Eckhart: "The more hooked you are on God, the more
> freedom you will experience."[1] Yesterday, as the network meeting
> started, I was not free. I was distressed, discouraged, fearful that
> the network was a failure after all, since few were there at the be-
> ginning—and the ones who came late were one-and-a-half hours
> late! How can we accomplish anything if people are not there? I
> tried to quiet my spirit in God without much success. The meeting
> turned out OK, but I see that I am far from the freedom Eckhart
> speaks about.

Early on, I learned sort of by accident that members of the network
were murmuring in their tents about me and my leadership. The problem,
I was told by a close friend and member, was money. Ah, money! Because I
am white, and closely associated with AEE who they thought had access to
all sorts of money, surely they would benefit financially from this network
arrangement. This awareness led to a serious conversation with Antoine
about expectations and how to position the network within AEE. It was
fairly murky—as the network wasn't exactly a work of AEE—they had no
funding or project related to it—and I, being AEE's protégée missionary,
had a peculiar relationship with AEE that affected the network in certain
ways. In the end, I was able to craft a statement that spelled out exactly what
AEE's relationship with me and the network was, and was not, and tried
to explain that the network was not primarily—if at all—about money.
Members were to think rather about what they could contribute to the network—in their time, ideas, prayers, and even contributions if they wanted
to go that route—rather than what they could get out of it monetarily.

This issue was only just laid to rest, or remained restless, I should say,
and came up often over the years. But we weathered it, and despite struggles
(and my attempts to kill the network!), it survived. Why did I want to kill
it not once but three times? Always it was the same. We'd come to a place
where my level of acceptance and patience would pretty much run out.
Members were great on talk about how they loved the network and wanted
it to be a part of their lives, but very short on commitment and action.
They would promise to carry out various programs (which *they* instituted,
not me), and then simply not show up. They would come hours late to

1. Bangley, *Nearer to the Heart of God,* 73–74.

meetings, or not come at all, and not text or call to explain their absence. I would play scolding mom, hauling one or the other into my office and sternly asking them what they thought they were doing by not following up on their stated convictions about the network—the result was always contrition, with promises never to do it again—but no lasting change ensued. I would teach from God's word, urging them to keep their promises and build the vision they all said they loved. No change. So, OK. It must be done, then, I thought. Put it out of its misery.

I tried that, but each time they were appalled. What? Stop the network? We love it! We'll do better, we promise. So sorry, Mom! So we'd reinvent the network. I'd encourage them to come up with ideas about how to keep themselves on track and accountable, and I even at one point built a rule (patterned after the Rule of Benedict) with their help and approval. We did everything we could think of, and nothing seemed to work, but each time I felt we were done—at least I was done—they would not have it.

When we came to a crisis, or a time of self-evaluation, everyone agreed they wanted to continue, but perhaps it would be good if I, as visionary, would somehow "cast the vision" for them more clearly, and *then* they would be able to do the work. Each time this happened, I did what I could to sharpen my vision, but I don't think that was really the problem. They wanted someone to carry them along, and I, being a *muzungu*—white person—should be the one to do so, preferably providing lots of money for them along the way. As for me, my vision entailed that *they* own the network.

I believe these crisis times were probably good for the network—helping us to reshape and mold the work more clearly. It was necessary in the first years to work hard against the hand-out mentality of some—not all—of the members. This ran as an undercurrent, subversively, throughout those first years. Those members clung to the notion that I must be holding out on them, since they weren't seeing any monetary benefit from being in the network. That had never been our intention, however. The network was meant to be a mutually encouraging partnership of like-minded organizations, sharing their lessons learned or struggles, and perhaps finding projects of mutual interest they could do together. Somehow, though, the idea permeated like yeast that I was holding out on them, and should be able to find money for them to carry out their ministries. Perhaps one difficulty with the network was that I tried to make it be more than it was, or could be. I was encouraged very much by people I talked to about it, especially Westerners, and it may have grown into something bigger in my own mind than could be supported by the facts.

The good stuff

In the meantime, in between these near failures, there were, in fact, good times—excellent times. In the early few years, for example, we mounted an extraordinary outreach program to street kids and churches, including a cultural exchange. I had discovered several local pastors who seemed willing to explore ways their congregations could be introduced to street kids and prostitutes as people of value, to be accepted and loved. In general, they are looked down upon, ignored, if not actively despised by the established churches. Together with these pastors and our network leaders, we put together a wonderful round-robin visiting tour. Each network ministry had their own choirs, drama or skit group, and traditional dance troupe. Our tour involved bringing various members' cultural groups into these participating churches, and giving them time to perform a number, and one of them to give a testimony about how God had met them, even though they were abandoned by the world around them. This was one of God's "good works" that we found to "walk in" (see Eph 2:10). I don't, of course, know if there was any lasting impact from these close encounters, but I believe the idea and its execution was from God.

We also had football (soccer) tournaments, one each year for three years, using the teams that members had developed. They had few balls, no uniforms, and not many pairs of shoes among them, and we did our best to find donors to help with equipment. There was one occasion I remember vividly, when we had been given an assortment of uniforms in various sizes. The uniforms had to be handed out and donned just before the match, and finding the right size for everyone was a hilariously chaotic scene. These matches were planned as a way of attracting other street kids' attention, and the gospel was preached on the pitch at half time. It was very hard and complex work putting these together, and nothing *ever* went according to plan. One time a coach simply refused to bring his girls team at the last minute. Wonderful and unflappable head coach Zed, who had one of the strongest sports ministries in the network, cobbled together a team from local street girls/prostitutes he managed to find in time. He ran a quick practice with them, and they were enthusiastic, if completely without skills in the game, but the tournament was saved.

A glimpse from an update from February 2007.

> My biggest challenge and joy is the continuing growth and health of the network of Christian associations working to help

vulnerable children and women. We meet weekly at the committee level, monthly for all members, and have a monthly prayer day. We are all at work on preparing a master proposal base, from which we will create a consolidated proposal to present to prospective donors. I continue to be amazed at how God leads us, me, in going forward. I keep doubting and fearing it will suddenly collapse, but it doesn't! With money donated by my church, we will hold training sessions on vision building and leadership, followed by trauma counseling skills, for the leaders of the associations in the network. We will also use some of that money to cover administrative expenses for one year. I bless First Presbyterian Church, Bellevue, for seeing far with me into the potential for this network and helping us in this concrete way.

One of the network member associations invited me to visit their new school, made possible by a small grant from AEE. It is held in a house, each room a classroom, and to see those kids (many who still live on the streets) so eager to learn even when they don't have enough to eat or any of the basic necessities of life, is moving and heartbreaking. There are three levels in the program designed by the government (but with no funding this year) to help older kids catch up at the primary level so they can be able to enter secondary school in the regular system. [This was the first Catch-up School started by our network, in the ministry of Alexis Ruhumuriza.] Blackboards are rippled and difficult to write on because of being repainted so many times. None of the kids have desks, only simple benches. Most are dressed in their street clothes (no uniforms), which have probably rarely been washed. They want to be in school almost more than they want to eat! We are continuing to seek money to support this program for all our network members.

Reason to complain?

We managed to survive for the first year, during which I had much to learn. I wrote an update musing on the nature and reason for complaining, seeking perspective. In this narrative the child with the cleft palate reappears.

"It's not in my job description!" "I didn't sign up for this!" Indignation, impatience, frustration—these are familiar to all of us, I'm sure. When things stretch me beyond my expectations, and beyond my strength, and when circumstances pop up that kidnap me into realms I never dreamed I'd enter, what do I do? Me, I complain! Or,

I try *not* to complain, but it's hard to squash the internal outrage. I can identify with those Israelites whom Moses led out of Egypt, supposedly setting them free, who kept running out of water and food, and who had to wander for forty years because they wouldn't trust God to deal with the giants in the land he wanted to give them. Well, I'm not sure I'd have done any better. I begin to realize why Scripture is full of exhortations and encouragement to hang in there, and "let perseverance finish its work so that you may be mature and complete, not lacking anything" (Jas 1:4).

Various culture clashes are often the cause of such impatience and complaining. *But,* when I consider the suffering of most of the people here, not to speak of the suffering of Christ, I can gain some perspective on my own discomforts. It may be difficult, frustrating, confusing, even nonproductive, but it isn't on the level of war losses and subsequent unresolved trauma. Not only do people still feel burdened by the ravages of widespread massacre involving friends, neighbors, family, and church leaders one against another, but they are burdened by poverty that seems intractable. We—missionaries, NGOs, churches, government—do everything we can to raise people up and set them on paths of productivity and dignity, but the poverty (and all its attending ills) grinds on.

Am I without hope? Let me observe the behavior of the people around me. They are continuing to try. They are ready to laugh, and, if they are believers, to praise God. They are committed to prayer and song. On the other hand, they are also often fatalistic and stoical. Not surprisingly, they have found a way to wall themselves in emotionally so as to withstand ongoing hardships and setbacks. Even among Christians there is this stoicism. But they persevere. I may think it's not in my job description to have to undergo various trials. But if I remember who wrote the job description, I end up humbling myself. God did not promise an easy path—far from it—but he did promise joy, peace, and abundant life. My charge each day is to "seek first the kingdom of God and his righteousness." I pray that I will be able to do this, to rejoice in God, whose character and intentions are loving and good, and to quiet my impatience in the face of almost constant reconfigurations of my expectations.

OK, the case in point at this moment is that we had a death in one of our network ministries. It was a baby born with cleft lip and palate, whose mom had struggled to keep her alive for about six months, but she couldn't feed well, and lost much weight. After almost dying, she was put on a special feeding regimen and gained enough weight to be operated on, but she didn't survive the operation. I went with her mother and friends who are helping her to get the baby's body released from the hospital. It was the second day we had gone. Sunday, they would not release the body because we couldn't pay the entire bill. The insurance company had not kicked in yet. We had to go away, after many hours of hassling and waiting, leaving the baby there, which made the mother terribly sad.

The next day, we returned to the hospital at about 9 a.m. The baby was not released to us until 8 p.m. Most of the intervening time was spent going from one office to another, being told we needed another document, and then another, which meant sending someone to the mother's village to get what was needed, and then at the end being refused the baby's body because we couldn't pay the whole amount that was left after the insurance paid their part. It turned out that the insurance hadn't been in place at the time the baby was admitted.

I spent the day alternately seething, brooding, praying, and just zoning out, in between asking fruitlessly what was going on, and trying to comfort the mom (Denise). No one seemed really to care about her. They care only about their so-called system, which is stressed terribly with not enough staff and too many people in need. At the end of the day, the mother went with her baby, laid in a small wooden casket we had bought in the morning, in a hired pickup with a small makeshift cross stuck above the cab and lights flashing, to burial—at night, and in a heavy rain. I left them to attend to another emergency. Another of our leaders had called earlier urgently requesting my help with money for medicine. She was seriously ill, I learned later, with some kind of kidney disease. I got to her house about 8:30 p.m., gave her some money, prayed, and went home exhausted and depleted in every way. Next day, I was told that Denise is now at peace, having buried her baby.

To set the captives free

One year we managed, with great difficulty and frequent setbacks, to do a ministry within a sort of prison. It was "sort of" a prison because it looked like a prison—grim walls, and inmates were locked up—but it was actually meant to be a temporary holding facility for street kids and other vagrants (including the ubiquitous street vendors of produce and garments who were on the street illegally) who would be swept up from time to time and taken into the buildings. There were thousands of these people. After being vetted by the police and prison authorities, our wonderful network members worked out a visiting and preaching schedule which I know touched many lives.

Once, it was my turn to preach. Patricia, whose ministry called Sowing Hope was one of the earliest members of the network, was to interpret. I faced a sea of young men, all seated on the cement floor in rows. Patricia had not told me she was going to ask me to preach, so this was very much a last-minute affair. But God met me powerfully, as he clearly did not want this opportunity to be wasted. I found myself telling them about the worst decision I had ever made—abandoning my children—and its terrible consequences. They were rapt—Patricia was doing an excellent job, flowing with me in interpreting—and then I told them about the best decision I had ever made: to follow Christ. When I finished, I asked if anyone who had never previously said yes to Jesus wanted to do so now. Instantly hundreds of hands shot into the air. It was a powerful and moving work of the Holy Spirit in these desperately needy young men's lives. Patricia and I led them in a prayer to receive Jesus, and I trust that God made at least some of them new creations in that moment.

In the last year before I returned to the states—although I hadn't yet made that decision—I decided to appoint a new leader to take my place, one of the members. When I told them my plan, they were delighted; it was clearly what they wanted, and was perhaps overdue. I prayed about this huge decision, but there was little doubt in my mind that only one person was mature and wise enough to take on leadership: Alexis. When I asked him if he would be willing to take this responsibility on, knowing well how full his life already was, he immediately said yes. It was clear to me that he alone knew how to build leadership, delegate authority, and develop a growing vision for the network.

The announcement of my choice was well-received by the members, and for a few months it appeared that new life was flowing in the network. However, circumstances conspired to force Alexis to leave Rwanda as a refugee in July 2015. A planned visit to his wife and children turned into an escape, as the government authorities tried to detain him. The reasons are complex and sensitive, but the outcome was that now the network was leaderless. Nevertheless, as I discuss in the section on my return to the United States, the network survived.

The network was, and continues to be, an uneven work of flawed people struggling to keep their own lives going while ministering to the desperately poor and lost street kids and prostitutes who are their beneficiaries.

The leaders continue to struggle to trust each other, to care for one another, and to hold onto the vision they profess to love too much to let go of. My thought is that with all its uncertainties and flaws, the network has been a good thing for members and their beneficiaries. As long as it lasts, it will do some good—visiting patients in hospitals, carrying the word of the Gospel to as many as possible in a variety of means and venues, and caring for one another. It is something to be glad for.

10

The Healing Crucible

IT IS CLEAR TO me that God used my being in Rwanda to bring about deep healing in me. It is as though Rwanda was his particular crucible, or instrument, to soften hardness and self-righteousness, judgmental spirit, and cultural/intellectual superiority, so I could not only be blessed in growing wholeness of soul, but also be able to bless others. The fault line along which healing was needed was the persistent theme of *mother*. Along the way, I was given tools to help others heal.

In the first year, there came a timely and helpful opportunity to attend a seminar called Ancient Paths. Created by Craig Hill from Colorado, the Ancient Paths seminar is based on Jer 6:16, which says, "This is what the Lord says: 'Stand at the crossroads and look; ask for the ancient paths, ask where the good way is, and walk in it, and you will find rest for your souls.' But you said, 'We will not walk in it.'" His thesis is that God has set forth in Scripture "ancient paths," which we are meant to find and walk in, that will assure God's blessing at the crucial stages of our lives, and ensure blessing for future generations—specifically regarding our destiny and our identity. He shows how God appointed "agents," called parents, to secure his blessings to children, and how at each stage of a person's life, from conception to old age, there are safeguards in place so that our identity and our destiny will be protected and nurtured.

The problems come when Satan sets up schemes—self-sustaining systems for cursing—that rob us of the blessings at various points in our lives. For me, the blessing of a mother was taken from me as an infant because my mother died when I was born, and the consequences of that have been long-lasting, compounded by the fact that I had a stepmother who failed to bless me. In the terms of the seminar, she was "hijacked by Satan," and invested considerable energy in cursing my identity and destiny. She told me repeatedly that I was worthless (identity), and would never amount to anything (destiny). I have learned that many people are under such a curse, some even from their own mothers.

What happens to a child who is robbed of *all* blessings, from conception onwards? The children of Rwanda who are sniffing glue and scrounging in trash heaps have been conceived in violence or fear or ignorance—certainly in poverty. Their time in the womb has been burdened by anxiety, not eager expectation, of the mother who carried them. Their birth was attended only by pain and fear, and they were either dumped into the arms of some barely willing relative or raised as a slave in their own homes, subject to beatings or molestation from drunken men who may or may not have been their fathers. Their passage into puberty was either unnoted or violent; certainly no one cared to tell them what was happening to their bodies, nor how God had made them for his good purpose. So they are poised for destruction in society; either they will self-destruct (suicide, alcoholism, glue-sniffing, or being killed in some criminal activity) or they will become time bombs. AIDS will spread among their sex partners (they are unlikely to ever actually marry), and the vile lies that Satan has established in their souls about their identity and destiny will be passed on to future generations.

In the course of the three days of the seminar, we met several times in a small group for ministry, with facilitators helping us to see where we had gone off track from the intended blessings at various points in our lives. Where there was some part we had played—perhaps in our marriage or as parents—we were invited to confess and repent, and receive God's forgiveness. Where there was damage in our own hearts because of missed blessing, we were invited to speak out our experience and our hurt, to the group, and then in prayer, to ask God to give us *now* what we had failed to receive *then*. The results were notable release in many cases from long-standing burdens and pain. In my case, I was finally able to make a good start at forgiving myself for my own failures as a mother, although I learned several years later that self-forgiveness had yet to be completed. This was the beginning for me to open the door to God to use me in the very domain of my failure, as a kind of "mother" in the latter part of my life.

I noted how Jesus was blessed and affirmed at all stages of his life, from his birth announcement to his baptism. ("This is *my* Son; in him I am well-pleased," blotting out all shame that might be attached to his "illegitimacy.") Jesus did everything out of the Father's blessing. God intends that everybody have such blessings, not just the Jews. He wants the ancient paths to be restored. Though the blessings were missed at their proper times, they can be restored now, through prayer.

Ways to enter in

I began to wonder how to bring these truths and blessings into the lives of street children, who so desperately needed them. I had gone from time to time to "preach" to them (share something of God's word), but often felt frustrated as it seemed only vaguely helpful, if at all. The problem was, perhaps, that I didn't really try to listen to God about what he wanted me to say to them. I saw that God was gently prodding me to enter in, to *see* them, try to understand who they were and what they longed for in life. Then perhaps I could speak into their lives in a helpful way.

My *muzungu* (white person) status could be either a hindrance or an asset. Seen as a source of money, I was a curse. But if the attention they gave me because I'm white helped them to hear a word of grace—just by virtue of their attentiveness—then being white could help, as a sort of "in."

God used that once in a slum where I was invited to come and preach. Unbeknownst to me, a young woman in that area, infamous for her screaming and bad behavior, who lived as a prostitute, had prayed that morning to get out of the life she was living. She prayed that if a *muzungu* would come that day and preach, she would give her life to the Lord and come out of prostitution. I was that *muzungu*! She began her journey into the light that day, although dazed by drunkenness and despair, and left the slum to get the help we offered. She might not succeed, however; the odds were against her. She needed to hear that God blesses her, heals her at every specific point of loss and damage, and to believe she is worth God's love. I wasn't able to follow up to know whether she stuck around long enough for God's servants to bring that message home to her.

So my question became, how to fold the truths of the Ancient Paths seminar into a way of working with street kids and prostitutes—perhaps not as a "program," but as a tool we could use to help pry open the closed and hardened hearts, damaged so severely by trauma at every point. If we could train several people to listen to the children, ask questions that would help them uncover their points of loss and pain, and lead them to pray for God's healing, we might be able to help many of those kids get back on track, into the destiny God has made them for.

I actually wrote up a plan to put this into action, but for various reasons I didn't put it into any sort of program. However, God used its teachings in various ways. For example, as I was still processing all the healing work God was doing in me, I had an opportunity to meet with a young man who has since become a "son" to me, called George. He came to my house just to visit with me, but ended up sharing about his wretched childhood, in which his father had abused him terribly, and virtually all the potential blessings were changed to curses, under which he was still suffering.

In a very tentative way, uncertain of how I could help, I shared some of the basic ideas about losing one's blessings in childhood, and thus growing up with a distorted idea of our identity and destiny. I invited him to share, as unto God, any feeling of loss and grief he wanted to share—and he did so, sobbing and crying out to God, telling him all his pain. As I waited beside him, I witnessed God's healing work begin to transform his grief. As I understood that his whole family was suffering, living in disharmony, I realized that they were all affected by the loss of blessing, and the cursing of identity by their father. It seemed to me that George, of them all, had a good chance of being the curse-breaker. And so it has turned out. He has reached many of his personal goals, confident in himself as God's beloved son, and his sisters have been blessed by his transformation.

Thirty-four orphans

Years later, another opportunity and calling had its roots in this teaching. One day as I was praying, I felt God nudging me to think about the thirty-four orphans in a village called Mukono, high in the mountains above the tea plantations where they often worked for daily wages. I had visited their village with Zed, a leader in the network, and was moved profoundly by the extraordinary beauty of this lofty village, with views all around, obscured then revealed by clouds. Far below, you could see brilliant green swathes of tea plantations where many of the children worked for pennies a day instead of going to school, so they could eat. The beauty lifted my heart, but it was marred—as everywhere in Rwanda—by the evidence of profound poverty. Villagers, including the children in child-headed homes, lived in huts made of mud, with a short-lived structure of reeds or sticks, most without doors, inner rooms, or windows. Often, a goat or sheep shared the shelter with the people.

Zed had familial connections there, and a strong relationship with the pastor who "ruled" over this region in genial and paternalistic fashion. Anything of a developmental nature that got done there was done with his help and approval. As I listened that day to God, I seemed to hear him tell me to go to that village and teach the elders to love the children in their midst. I was surprised; I thought, "That can't be right—that's too simple. Surely they don't need anyone to teach them to love the orphans." But this was a very insistent nudge, and I felt I had to follow it up.

After sharing the idea with Zed, and then with the local pastor, the idea began to take shape as a real need and ministry. It developed into a two-day seminar, given to selected adults in the community whom the pastor had decided could commit to such a plan and program. We put together a simple curriculum on how to love the children. Again and again I felt uncertain—wouldn't they already know what we were going to teach them? As it turned out, they did not know. As we shared on such subjects as listening to the young people, asking them how they are doing each day, spending a little time with them, we kept seeing the adults' amazed faces, as they took these things in, which seemed new to them. And I think they were new; as we discovered, they themselves had likely not had anyone to love them in these simple ways, no one who had seen them as valuable human beings.

In the Rwandan culture, children are not usually valued as themselves, as persons, but rather, as workers and helpers in the house and garden, from the very earliest age. No one thinks to ask a child what he is thinking, or how he feels, or what his hopes and fears might be. These are simply irrelevant. Yet, the adults listened like sponges. Clearly this was a work of the Holy Spirit, laying a groundwork and seeds of a whole new mentality for the adults regarding the children in their midst.

The culmination of the event was a teaching time on the events and effects of puberty, and how the adults could best love the young people as they go through that crucial transition. As I listened to the woman who was teaching about this, I felt another inner nudge: it occurred to me that these adults might never have had anyone to teach *them* about what happens in puberty and the time leading up to marriage—the "facts of life." I decided to interrupt the lecture and ask the group how many had no one to help them through this time. Almost all hands went up. I wept for the loss this represented in their lives. Every one of these adults had lived right through the enormous and mysterious changes of adolescence and courtship and marriage without a single person to tell them what was going on, or to share knowledge and wisdom with them. They had endured all kinds of superstitious stories. One prevalent myth was that if a girl got pregnant without being married, she would be thrown into a lake. Girls had tried to teach each other from what their aunts may have told them—mostly in ignorance. It was an eye-opening experience, and very moving. Every person there wanted to tell about what had happened to them during that time. Every one. The stories were heartbreaking, but it was also clear that what we were doing might go far to break the generational cycle of cursing, and to actually accomplish some healing of those hearts that had been so wounded.

That "love program" has taken hold and persisted years along, according to Zed's reports. A tiny nudge from God, a "whisper" as Bill Hybels likes to say, and God took a small village in hand for his blessing and healing.

Working it out

In February of 2006 I was again struggling with the strong emotions of guilt and grief over how I had damaged my children.

> The pain continues—not all the time, but then something triggers it, as I thought this morning that God does not ever withhold his love, regardless of my behavior, as he is the best parent—and the pain rose up and engulfed me. So here is a word to instruct me: "Through love and faithfulness sin is atoned for; through the fear of the Lord evil is avoided" (Prov 16:6) Another version has "loyalty and faithfulness." Jesus' own loyalty and faithfulness on the cross have atoned for my sins—*but* this is also the way my life must be: to, in a sense, "work out my own salvation in fear and trembling"—by love and loyalty (which has to do with service, allegiance, sticking to the one I serve and not going elsewhere) and faithfulness. Obedience day after day, staying lined up with God's purposes.

As I returned to this guilt many times, it appeared also that God wanted to take me further along in my own healing as a failed mother. Not only did I receive help through the ministry of the Ancient Paths seminar, but God led me into two distinct and necessary identifications with grief, which brought me to a deeper level of understanding of the nature and consequences of my decision to leave my children so long before. The first part was a period of grieving for my own loss, in having left my children. By God's gracious and insistent hand, I was shown what was in my heart. I had missed out on so much! They had all been under eleven years old at the time. Still little girls, filled with the curiosity of discovering their world and themselves, and navigating all the challenges of elementary school, homework, parent meetings—without me. I missed sharing all that with them, and watching them grow into young ladies. I had never thought about my own grief in this way before, and it was painful. But I also knew that since I had not been the one to initiate this time of grieving, God was using it for my healing.

The second part—I don't recall how much time elapsed between the two—was to enter into *their* grief. Up to that time I had mostly struggled with my guilt and shame; that had been the major burden for me. But now God wanted to help me participate in some measure in their own grief— what it was like for them to lose their mom while she was yet alive. About that time, I can say only that the grief was deep and real, but I know too that it was only a taste of what they suffered. I am glad my God took me through that, and out the other side. He clearly didn't want me wallowing in either sort of grief, but rather to taste it, and then to be able to set it in its place among the experiences of my life. I am always amazed when I think these things happened while I was in Rwanda, so far from my girls. In this sense, Rwanda has been a healing place for me.

A new understanding

Toward the end of my time in Rwanda, I began attending seminars of Ellel Ministries,[1] including teachings on how God wants to heal deep wounds from our past—often as a result of unhealthy or ungodly bonds (Ellel uses the term "soul-ties") with people. After one such training, I took time to pray about my relationship with my father. As I have said, my father was a strong but distant figure in my life. As a child, and later as an adult, I always wanted him to be proud of me, but never felt I succeeded in that goal. Dur-

---

1. Ellel Ministries is a nondenominational, international ministry that uses biblical resources for inner healing, and teaches others to do so, through training and workshops. https://peterhorrobin.com/ellel-ministries/.

ing the prayer time I realized there were two specific things I needed to forgive my father for: One was when he told me he would have divorced my stepmother if it were not for my sister Deborah (his daughter with my stepmother). He could not bear the thought of leaving her. Leaving me, or my brother, apparently would not have been a problem. Those words hurt me, although I never told him so.

The second thing I remembered that I needed to forgive him for also had to do with my sister. When my stepmother was dying, I was traveling from California, where I had just graduated from Santa Clara University, to Seattle to start graduate studies. In Eugene, Oregon, I had stopped for a few days to attend the wedding of a friend, and I was there when Daddy called to say my stepmother was nearing the end of her life. I asked him if I should come (they lived in Pennsylvania at the time), and he said no, "Don't come; I have Deborah here, and she is taking care of everything." To my subsequent shame and grief, I didn't go, and needed to deal with that as another issue. But here was another hurtful word showing me my father's clear preference for my sister, and also his complete disregard for me.

As I began to ponder these things, ready to forgive him, another memory came strongly to mind. Whenever I had asked Daddy to tell me something—anything—about my mother who had died at my birth, he refused, saying he couldn't remember anything. Finally, I asked him one day to tell me how my mother had died, as no one had ever explained the circumstances to me. He received this request with something that looked to me like disgust, and then said OK, he would tell me, but I was never to raise this question again. Then he told me she had died from pneumonia resulting from aspirating some vomit during labor. As I write this now, I realize even that doesn't seem like enough information—why would she have vomited? But that was all I got from him. Remembering this while in prayer, I suddenly had a clear understanding—I believe revealed to me by God—that my father had totally rejected me from the moment of my mother's death. He never accepted me as his daughter. When I saw this, it was as though many things fell into place. I could see the whole range of distancing my father practiced, and understand it from this new perspective. Of course he never showed any affection, or took me on his lap, or told me he loved me. He could not. I was simply not his daughter, but rather a painful reminder of his wife who died.

With the tears of understanding came also a flood of compassion for my poor father. What a miserable time he had! Not only was he married to a woman who had turned out to be a very great trial to him—treating him often with great contempt and sarcasm, even as she also treated me. And now I think I was able to understand why he never interceded for me when she treated me cruelly—he was as much a victim as I was. Not only so, but he had also to live with me, this living reminder of his lost wife, who in retrospect must have glowed in memory compared to the woman he ended up with.

As a result of these penetrating insights from God, I had no trouble forgiving my father, and thanking my heavenly Father for revealing this to me at the right time. I felt that I would now be learning more—able to receive more—about God's Father heart, and also able to minister with more compassion to the many, many others whose fathers have rejected them in one way or another, including my own daughters.

11

Stress and Growth

MY SPIRITUAL LIFE HAS always been a collage, or a patchwork, with only dimly discernible patterns. We used to have quilts at home when I was growing up that were made by grandmothers, called crazy quilts. They were pieced together from rags, leftover scraps from sewing projects, or donated odds and ends. There was no particular design that one could see. I suspect this is a true picture of many people's spiritual journey. The road we're on is not clearly marked out for very far ahead at any one time, since we *are* meant to walk by faith, not by sight. I think God is committed to teaching us to learn this, and to grow in faith.

The bright patches in my quilt are blessedly frequent: they are the moments of peace and joy, or of exaltation in praise and awareness of God's goodness and love. They include precious insights into his word, direction along the path, and quietness and rest. They also include intimate openings into the heart of God, signaled to me by tears as I pray. The dull patches, the less attractive bits (like old, worn-out clothes cut up to fill in the spaces between the pattern pieces), are moments or days of discouragement, despair, apathy—or worse, complacency. They include stretches of deliberate attempts to distract myself from the things and purposes of God.

The bridging pieces—are they bright and shining, or commonplace gingham?—are times of restoration through self-awareness and repentance. I love the place in Second Peter where he says that there are two "keepings": our salvation is being kept in heaven for us (that's God's promise and assurance), but even more wonderful, we are kept, also by God, for that salvation while we are on earth. God does it all. (See 2 Pet 1:3–5)

Growing self-awareness

Over the years I have had emotional struggles connected with a sense of inadequacy, often expressed as a need for more love, both from God and for others. As I was throwing myself into a variety of ministries to women and children at risk—people who because of their own lacks and needs were often not lovable in obvious ways—I became aware of my own lack of love, and often turned to God about this. More than once, I recalled the dearth of love from my parents—especially my father—as a child.

One manifestation of inadequacy was probably my tendency to take on much more than I ought to have done, with the result that I felt overloaded and even resentful at times. I seemed to feel that I needed to try everything that presented itself, since I was never sure what I was supposed to do. As a result, I had a heavy teaching load along with my responsibilities to the network I had formed early on, and to AEE who was my umbrella organization in Rwanda. I also formed financial dependency relationships with several people—not all of these probably bad, but I later imagined I may have taken on more people to support through school or other personal goals than was wise.

In the midst of all this was a pretty much continuous engagement with one housemate after another. These people were part of the cultural environment in which I was being honed spiritually; each of them had come to Rwanda with her own agenda and issues. The culture interacted with these in various ways, sometimes with unpleasant or painful effect, and I felt a kind of mentor/mom responsibility to all of them (whether rightly or wrongly). I was both blessed and stretched in these relationships.

An overarching and also underlying element throughout was the culture challenge. I was diligent from the start in studying Kinyarwanda—which I loved—and in my studies, I felt God giving me much help. In my multitudes of interactions with Rwandese, I was learning about the significant differences between my culture and theirs. I was trying to figure out how best to engage with this culture, which often was inexplicable and even unattractive to me, without losing my identity. At some point I came to the helpful realization that I would always be an American, and that the best I could do would be to understand where people in Rwanda are coming from, and how their culture informs their behavior. I would seek to come alongside in whatever ways seemed to be useful and helpful. I would never change anyone, nor would I change much, culturally. The only changes I could count on would be inner, or spiritual, as a result of my or others' encounters with God. I often encountered visitors, or even other cross-cultural workers in Rwanda, who liked to make sweeping generalizations about "those people." I resisted the temptation to characterize all Rwandese, but sometimes it was difficult not to apply certain observations to the general population.

Breaking down

The stresses of being in and having to interact with another culture were probably more than I realized. I imagine I expected too much of myself—as well as of others—in the early years. And there was also the burden of others' expectations of me—especially as a Westerner, who was therefore rich. I was constantly, daily, exposed to people who one way or another were demanding "their" money from me. Since I obviously had money, some of it must be theirs. I didn't understand this thinking, but I saw it often. Children in particular would holler at me as I passed in my car, "Give me my money!" Since I was giving away quite a lot of money, but of course couldn't explain that to any given person on the street, this was difficult for me to deal with emotionally. And all around me people were suffering and dying. I came to dread phone calls. Who was sick now? Whose burial would I have to attend now? It wore on me emotionally, even as I sought God for the love and mercy I needed to meet these dark challenges.

Here are lines I wrote reflecting on these struggles:

More love for these, O Christ, more love for these!

- The child who comes up to my window as I try to enter traffic: "give me money! I'm hungry!"
- The driver who steers his car around the whole waiting line of cars to be first.
- The woman whose legs are stumps with feet attached, scooting along with her bottom brushing the ground.
- The suave businessman with jewelry and pointy shoes and large belly.
- The pastor who can't help whining because she sees so little hope.
- The slick street boy who demands to guard my car.
- Sauntering women in four-inch heels, high breasts, and bare shoulders.
- The poorest mothers with babies on their backs without protection from the sun, or flies, or dust.

- All who stare at me, and stare, and never look away.
- All who yell "muzungu!"
- All worshipers whose amplified preaching and prayer disturbs my sleep.

More love, O Christ for these! More love for Thee.

Not surprisingly, I broke down every now and then. I just felt I had come to the end of myself and my strength and couldn't do it anymore. It is possible these times may have been, in part, symptomatic of the general lack of clarity, certainty, or direction I was living with. Once a person knows what they are supposed to do, and where they are supposed to go, other things can fall into place or fall by the wayside as irrelevant. On further reflection, though, I believe such times as these were inevitable, understandable, and quite common. The great wonder is that God consistently brought me through them well.

Part of what was going on in these dark times was the work of healing God was doing in me, which I discuss elsewhere. It may well be that the brokenness I experienced in myself as a result of the pressures and burdens I describe, as well as that brokenness which I observed in others, was the matrix in which God could show his intentions for wholeness in every aspect of my life. I talked with many friends in Rwanda who said much the same thing happened to them, and they learned such deep things about themselves and God as they never thought of before.

For all this miserable, limping, scattered life I was leading, God sustained me. I know this is so because surely I would have long since given up and returned to America, or I would have succumbed to serious mental or other illness. Except for the brief breakdowns, and waves of depression that I have experienced over the years, I never felt discouraged enough to give up and leave Rwanda until time to do so. I was also never seriously ill, except for one bout with relatively mild pneumonia.

Faith sustained

God sustained me in these ways, but more importantly, or perhaps because, he sustained me in faith. It seems logical that I would grow at least dim or dull in my belief and trust in God, or at worst, bitter and cynical. But that never happened. On the contrary, I maintained—purely by God's grace—a regular and rich discipline of Bible study and prayer, as well as times of worship. I read my Bible with my journal by my side, and often wrote about what I read, allowing God's spirit to direct me to connections with other places in the Bible or other ideas that would often amaze and delight me. Since I have for many years followed the Robert M'Cheyne Bible reading guide,[1] I have returned again and again to all parts of the Bible—each time discovering passages anew, or renewing my special friendship with them. As I was also writing in my journal daily, I kept close to God in relating what I had experienced and how it affected me, and what I thought I was supposed to be learning from it. So I had God as my steady guide and companion all along the way.

A powerful way God also sustained me was in giving me opportunities to teach and preach; in each case I would need to seek him about what to teach, or if I had a specific assignment, how to teach. I felt regularly enriched and delighted by the ways God met me for these tasks—often very much at the last minute, or in ways I wouldn't have expected.

God sustained me in giving me friends. At times my roommates became special friends, but more often I found friends among the expat community who assembled regularly for fellowship and worship. At first I kept myself aloof from expats, because I had a rather lofty idea that as a missionary I needed to associate only with the people I came to serve. But I well remember the first time I decided to attend an expat Bible study/fellowship on a Sunday afternoon. Almost the moment I walked into the hosts' lovely home, I knew I had been missing something very important. As much as I wanted to be totally committed to Rwandans, and to serve them with love and compassion, I realized I needed a place to be myself, and to be able to share with other Westerners from around the world experiences of being stationed in Rwanda. Many came for a long-term commitment; more came for a limited time. But I saw that I needed this fellowship and support, and quickly made good friends with those who came week after week. We shared our gifts, our challenges and questions, and most of all the fellowship of Christ. We laughed and cried together, prayed with each other through all kinds of difficulties and frustrations, and learned from each other.

Even while I could see many ways God worked to sustain, protect, and lead me into new understanding, I also saw that I am always a journeyer— my email name is Sojourning—and had a very long way to go. I still needed God's prompting to show love and compassion when my natural response was to withhold myself from a need that might suck me into it beyond my

---

1. Haslam, "Robert Murray M'Cheyne's Bible Reading Calendar."

capacity. This is nothing other than a fear of losing control, so I had to keep remembering I was not in control of outcomes or the future, only of my responses and decisions in the current situation.

Still today I succumb to moments of overwhelming sadness—forgetting, in the practical working of faith, that my God is carrying all the burden of the world's suffering. I came to realize that I need to share in his sufferings, as Paul understood. As we have "hope of the glory of God," he says in Rom 5:2, he continues, "Not only so, but we also glory in our sufferings, because we know that suffering produces perseverance . . . hope" (Rom 5:3–4). The connection between the hope we Christians have in sharing in God's glory and suffering is threaded throughout Scripture—I think particularly of Paul's words in Rom 8:17, "Now if we are children, then we are heirs—heirs of God and co-heirs with Christ, *if indeed we share in his sufferings in order that we may also share in his glory*" (emphasis mine).

I find it very helpful, not only for myself when suffering in some way, but also in listening to another's tale of suffering, to remember this connection between our sufferings and the suffering of Christ. It lifts our spirits, even though the suffering is intense, to know it is part of Christ's suffering. The reason is that Christ did not suffer in vain; so if our suffering is linked with his, there is a redemptive quality or aspect to it. God sees our sufferings, takes note of them, and promises his presence and protection in the midst, and he "will raise us up at the last day" (John 6:39, 40, 44, 54).

From busy, to being

Toward the end of my time, I became aware of a new perspective on those early years in Rwanda, in which I was always very busy, and so keen on being involved in many ministries. As my journals reveal, I was also frequently afflicted with many doubts about my purpose, and fell often into periods of despair. The perspective I came to, not long before I left the country, is that perhaps all my busyness was not necessarily what God had in mind. I am sure he was at work in much of it, and many worthwhile things came into being. But now that because of my increasing age I was no longer able to run here and there, no longer up to the kind of pace I once led, I thought that perhaps I had got it wrong from the beginning. God invited me to go to Rwanda to live. That was it. It was I who felt I had to come up with some justification for being here, and find my identity through all the work I was doing. People always asked, "So, what do you *do* here?" How could I just say, "Well, you see, I live here." But in the last couple of years that was pretty much it. I lived there. I am a human being, as the saying goes, not a human doing. I still had things to do—but I was in a restful mode. I could see people who wanted to get together to talk, encourage, or counsel as the opportunity arose—rest and read and pray.

Prayer is necessary to my life. I wish I could say that I pray without ceasing, but that is not the case. Still, the times I do pray—early in the morning while reading my Bible or other good writing, and journaling—are often intense, filled with weeping for the pain and suffering of the world, and primarily intercessory. But I also often feel the need to review before God the way I have come with him, how I got here, and what he has done so far—and where I hope to be going. As the world seems to be darker and heavier with wickedness, I long for the return of the King. But I know he will come at the right time, and wants to find me faithful, ready, and obedient. So prayer also has this dimension—asking God to keep me on the right way, to guard my heart from becoming bitter, cynical, hard, and to sustain me in whatever he has for me to be and do.

12

Reflections on Ministry in the Culture of Rwanda

Bridge the gap

I didn't understand a thing in church today,
I missed the numbers of the hymns,
I couldn't catch the Scripture references.
The choirs sang with child-like gestures
all in vain; I couldn't grasp their words.

I committed to this Presbyterian church.
The pastor even came to visit me,
and blessed me with a prayer—
I like the spirit here, the welcome, and the dancing.

But I cannot get the message, nor worship freely.
I'm often preaching at some other church.
I'm still the one and only white, most times,
and made aware of this by people's stares.

I can work hard, my choice, to bridge the gap.
Jesus did, though no one understood him;
he made the leap and learned our language.
Compared to that, Kinyarwanda is a snap.

SO MUCH HAPPENED IN the first year I was in Rwanda: I learned Kinyarwanda well enough to preach a sermon to a group of street kids in March. I found and furnished a house. I bought a little RAV4 and started driving. I had been terrified of the prospect, but once I got behind the wheel I was calm and felt confident. I wondered why I had been so afraid! I met and became close to a number of ministry leaders, and began investing myself in their work. I was writing proposals for projects for AEE, and one of those proposals was funded. Thus, in conjunction with AEE, I started the project of bringing a mobile clinic to various sites visited by network member Muhumurize's beneficiaries—street kids and very poor men and women—which ran for several years with some good effect.

My ministry continued to grow in the unique context of Rwandan culture, as I learned about myself in relation to Rwandese coworkers and friends, and learned slowly about our many significant differences. Some degree of frustration is evident in these brief lines:

Formalities

Everything must be stamped or no one takes you seriously.
Put your request for rubber bands in writing, please,
on letterhead. Stand in *that* line, over there,
and when you reach the *guichet*, the lady says,
not glancing up: Go away! Come back tomorrow!

People love to say what's what,
even when they're ignorant. They're quick to say:
Not possible, not available, can't be done.
But sometimes, a bureaucrat shows he's human,
willing to listen, look at your document,
give you what you need. A rare find!
Get his number—you may need it down the line.

Going along in this rhythm of exploring, studying, learning about the culture and the language, I was also discovering a key principle of life. It's not easy! So many people have mused and written and theorized about this fact, that it seems almost silly to mention it. Nevertheless, I think each of us has to realize the truth of it in our own way. It should never be a surprise or a shock to us when we run into roadblocks or painful experiences along the way. We are not greater than our master, nor than our great forbears in the Christian experience. What I would love for myself, and my fellow journey-ers, would be a kind of exuberance that recognizes every day the possibil-ity—even probability—that something will come up to cause derailment, distraction, distress, pain, or just plain annoyance. We could make our way through life so much more joyfully if we could just say, "Of course!" Jesus said, "In the world you will have trouble," but he also said, "But take heart! I have overcome the world."

The "not easy" aspect of living and serving in Rwanda had mostly to do with the radically different mind-set of many Rwandese. In many cases, their responses to life situations ran counter to my normal responses. I was likely to do a fair bit of wailing, complaining, or indulging in self-pity before coming around to trusting God. Not so with many Rwandese. With them there is a general acceptance—sometimes fatalistic or stoic—of all manner of obstacles or disappointments. The generic and widespread response to all of these is "*Wihangane!*" which roughly translated means "hang in there, be patient." And here is where my spiritual challenge came: It's all very well if people want to tell themselves to hang in there, but I got so I hated to hear that word as a response to *my* struggles or pain! I couldn't appreciate the fact that others weren't taking my struggle or difficulty as seriously as I thought they should. I had trouble understanding what may be a true strength of the Rwandan character: Whenever they meet various trials, if they are Christians, they are generally ready to "hang in there"—trust God with the hardship, and wait for him to see them through it. Then, when he does, they will "testify"; these testimonies include the whole story of the trouble, danger, trial, or whatever, so that when God's deliverance comes, it can be truly appreciated and God is praised exuberantly.

And their lives are so often really hard! They are generally poor—just barely managing to find the basic necessities of life. Even those who have jobs have a great many demands on their income, especially from extended family, many of whom may not have jobs. It is the eldest's responsibility to see the younger ones through school and married. Medical expenses are always lurking, as sickness is prevalent and medical care is at a low level compared to the Western world. Luxuries such as books or vacations, or children's toys, are mostly forgone (except for the minority well-to-do). Most people do have phones—as keeping in touch is essential—and many have TV sets, even if they can't manage to send their children to school. Beer and alcohol are abused widely, as are spouses. Life is extremely hard. Church is often the only outlet for many people, a place where they can let their hair down in extended prayer sessions and lots of hymn singing. The gospel truth about being "born again" or "saved" is often far from people's understanding, and there is a bizarre mix of hedonistic, flagrantly sinful lifestyles (adultery, drunkenness, lying, and slandering others, etc.) with the outward appearance of spirituality one sees in the churches.

Jealousy and sheer cussedness is a dark thread in this culture—and all Rwandese I have talked to agree that this is so. Jealousy rises up so easily and often that it just seems a normal part of the fabric of life. It happens everywhere. In ministry, for example, if a leader manages to do well in raising up a useful and fruitful work, one of that ministry's members is likely to start a rumor about the leader which, though untrue, will destroy the person's reputation, and then the slanderer will simply take over the ministry. We saw this happen twice within the network.

People are quick to believe slander and rumors—they are somehow delicious morsels. Jealousy destroys families. One member can have some success in business, or get a special opportunity from a friend, and other members will find a way to rob that person of the blessing. Jealousy and envy go hand in hand. Anyone who has something another does not is a likely target for attack. The result of this general unraveling of the material of common life is a widespread distrust. There is much suspicion of others; one can never trust what will happen to any shared confidence. Maybe the person who hears it will publish it broadly, and it will come back in hurtful ways. Best not to share at all.

Coming into this culture as a missionary/outsider, I had to learn how people think, and therefore act. I had to lay aside my prized Western logic and convictions and come alongside people to see how they really are, where their hearts are—and this was extremely difficult when most people fiercely guard their hearts so as not to be betrayed. One year, during the week that kicks off the one hundred days of mourning to commemorate the 1994 genocide, I decided to invite my network members to my home for a day of sharing and prayer. I tried to provide a comfortable and open atmosphere—including putting mats and mattresses on the floor as is common when there is a gathering for extended prayer. At some point after sharing from the word of God, I asked them if they would like to say anything about their experience or from their heart concerning the geno-cide—knowing that many people never do so, either because they are too traumatized to talk about it, or because they mistrust their hearers' inten-tions concerning what they might share. As it turned out that day, everyone did share, but the most moving was from Safari, a Hutu, who talked about what it was like for him, when everyone blamed the Hutus for the mas-sacres. He'd had no part in them, but his relatives had, and had been im-prisoned. This was a terrible burden to bear alone, and he had borne it until that day. He had never before dared to talk about his feelings or experience in a "mixed" group such as we were, and he said he was greatly relieved, and felt a burden lifted.

There is much more one could say about the difference in mind-set between Rwandese and Westerners—or at least me, but what came up for me most often was the way Rwandese process information. The direct ques-tion Westerners tend to ask is answered in such a roundabout way that often one is not sure it in fact *was* answered. The inquiry about what happened, or where someone was—simple enough from my point of view—would be answered by circumlocution. It was often quite baffling. I had to go after the information I needed from several different directions before I felt quite sat-isfied I had an answer somehow related to the question I asked. In general, as has been noted by many, Africans tend to think and talk in indirect, circular (or perhaps spiral) ways, and often involving lots of details that to a West-erner seem extraneous. As for me, I want to rush the speaker: get to the point, please! But that never works. He will arrive there in his own way, having thor-oughly explained everything he feels is relevant. In any case, I'm not sure "the point" is a goal for many Africans; the story, or the journey, is the goal.

I learned that I would never be able to think like a Rwandese—it just wouldn't happen. But to the extent I could at least try to understand why Rwandese speak the way they do, I could come closer to sharing my hu-manity with them—the ways we are the same. Paul said he had learned to become as all people so that he might somehow save some, and that was key in Rwanda, for sure. I suspect I was, even after many years in that culture, still stuck in my own ways of thinking and conversing—especially if there was urgency, or I was impatient. It was good to remember that God's grace does come in and ease many such fraught communications battles.

Invited to preach

In Rwanda, if you are a missionary—or even just a white person who is a Christian—you are invited to preach. Doesn't matter whether you have any knowledge of the Bible, or any preaching skills or calling. You are assumed to have something worthwhile to share, if you are a Christian. This is especially true if you come from the West, where everyone knows there is so much more knowledge and wisdom and learning than in Rwanda. Of course, many Westerners are quite varied in their knowledge of the Bible, and in their ability to expound upon it. But this was my strength, I felt. From the moment I recognized that Jesus was my Savior and in charge of my life, I had the desire to learn and to teach the Bible. I was trained, and had a lot of practice in the states teaching the Bible (there, one generally doesn't preach unless one is an ordained pastor). So it seemed quite a reasonable thing for me to do, when asked: will you come and preach on Sunday? Never mind that I had never before preached a sermon—I could do this! I think I was so excited to be asked, and to be able to pray and ask God what he might have for me to share with those people, that I didn't really consider how ill-equipped I was. I believe God was very kind and patient, and did meet me and use me on many of these occasions. But other times, I would come away with a falling sensation within—I had surely failed to edify anyone!

Once I had been asked by a member of the AEE staff to come to his church. I had an interpreter named Simon (at that time I was not yet able to preach in Kinyarwanda), a soldier, whom I had met on another occasion. As I preached, and Simon struggled to interpret (he seemed to have a great difficulty understanding what I was saying), I knew this was not working. It was only slogging to get through. Afterward, not one single person spoke to me (which is extremely rare—usually people will greet the preacher and other leaders as they leave the church). I left with my tail between my legs, sure I had failed utterly. Then I heard Simon's voice behind me, calling to me. As he came up to me, he told me with great earnestness that my sermon had been especially meaningful to him, and he was very thankful for it. Whether or not he heard what I was saying, or something entirely different that God was speaking into his heart by means of my words, I don't know. But I felt lifted up. One person had been somehow blessed, and so that was OK.

On another occasion, Annie of Green Pastures asked me to come help with a Sunday service to be held in the midst of a community where prostitutes and bar-owners lived. It turned out to be a meeting in a sort of open courtyard, in a very poor and miserable slum area. Normally, there was a pastor who gave the talks at these meetings, but at the very last minute it turned out he hadn't come, and I was pressed into service to preach. I had nothing prepared. I was not able to preach in Kinyarwanda. But truly God met me and lifted me up into a very powerful sermon which began in the Garden of Eden and ended somehow at the cross and resurrection of Christ. Many of the people who listened made a decision to turn their lives around, and let Christ be their Lord. One of these was a young bar-manager named Apolline (a woman), who also served as a pimp. She turned to the Lord, left her bar, and joined Green Pastures. Apolline never looked back. She went through extremely tough times, including being abandoned by Annie who had promised to help her and provide for her until she could get a job. But she told me later that she had committed her life to Christ that day, and nothing was going to discourage her from following him. She eventually became an excellent seamstress, got her own little space in Kigali, and became one of the Serena Hotel's major suppliers of uniforms. She traces her salvation back to that day when I spoke about the saving power of Christ. I had not prepared anything, but God was prepared to welcome her into his kingdom.

It often was the case that God used my testimony—as terrible as the prelude was—to touch people I preached to. I had to learn to humble myself, set aside my training and expertise in the Bible (God could use all that if he wished), and just tell my story, within whatever framework the particular preaching event called for. And I also had to learn—and never learned it well—that in Rwanda it is not principles or logical, abstract concepts that will take hold in people's hearts and minds, but rather, story, illustrations, drama—these are the materials of the African culture (mostly non-literate) that convey meaning. As an intellectual Westerner, I had a terrible time with this. I kept thinking I could just explain something, step by step, and it would be clear. But rarely was that the case. It is wonderful that Jesus was born into a similar culture, agriculturally based, and story-based, so that Rwandans are easily able to understand *him* if he is faithfully preached. He used all these story elements—parables, metaphors, similes, narration—to communicate the deepest truths. There were mill stones and vineyards, labor practices and children, wells and olive trees, birds and flowers—all part of his material for teaching in ways that would have remained on the inner eyes of his hearers.

Not only was I asked to preach, but also—quite frequently—to teach. Here I felt I could make freer use of my training—I loved to teach from the Bible using expository methods. I taught in contexts of various churches, as well as a group of intercessors whose leader wanted them to be soundly based in Scripture. I taught series: Romans, Revelation, Acts, Hebrews, and others. I also taught themes: prophecy, reconciliation, family life. I amassed many notebooks filled with teaching notes and outlines—but I never felt I could reuse any of them; each teaching situation called for its own research and preparation. So I was always learning and being stretched.

It occurred to me very late that I did not have anyone over me to whom I could be accountable in all this preaching and teaching activity. My pastor was Rwandese, and I had a limited relationship with him. My pastor in America was in America. To be sure, my background and training did put me ahead of most Rwandese in terms of Bible knowledge, and perhaps my age and experience counted for something. It is also true that various pastor friends who invited me to preach would sometimes offer critiques or advice. I hope and trust that God was always leading and guiding me—but it would have been better if I had found a mentor to stay close to.

Missing the meaning

Although I rarely repeated a teaching, my theme was often somehow the same: growing in Christ. In Rwanda there is a very great deficit of serious discipleship. While a high percentage of the people would say they are "saved," an almost equal percentage continue to live their lives as though nothing more were expected or required of them after choosing in some public meeting or "crusade" to receive Christ. It is evident in the way people live. Domestic violence has increased in a major way in the years following the 1994 genocide. There are frequent occurrences of poisonings or witchcraft curses, which kill people or seriously injure them, stemming from jealousy because of others' good fortune. Also, people consistently refuse to take any responsibility for their errors, mistakes, or delays. There is always an excuse, always someone or something to blame.

It was challenging to speak into such a culture in which people think of themselves as "saved" and yet are blind to the true meaning of being saved. There is truly a veil over people's minds. One can speak of the need to come out of sin, to refuse to recognize the demands of the flesh and to be led by the Spirit until one is blue in the face, and all hearers will nod and say amen and continue in their unregenerate ways.

When I taught, I always wanted both to point people to Jesus and to encourage them to look at their lives in the light of what Jesus said and did.

I've already said that I never taught in a new setting without including at least some of my own story of sin and redemption. I never wanted to give anyone the idea that I thought myself better or more spiritual than others. But I did want to call people—as well as myself—to the high calling of holiness I see in the Bible. A persistent theme for me, both in personal growth and in teaching, comes from Gal 5:1, "It is for freedom that Christ has set us free. Stand firm, then, and do not let yourselves be burdened again by a yoke of slavery."

I am thankful for all these opportunities God gave me to grow in my gifts, and to carry to many words of encouragement. I started without awareness of a gift for preaching; by the time I left Rwanda, it was clear that God had taken my ineptness—with my willingness—and equipped me for his service. All praise and honor to him!

13

The Return

THE QUESTION EVERYONE KEPT asking since I first went to Rwanda was, how long will you stay? Do you think you will ever return to the states? Will you die and be buried in Rwanda? I never knew how to answer these questions. I didn't know. I felt I wanted to leave that up to God, and trusted that somehow he would reveal to me if, or when, I should return to America. Meanwhile, I put things in order for my death in Rwanda, if that should happen. I made sure the people at AEE, my daughters, my friend who was my power of attorney, and others close to me knew what arrangements I had made—a simple burial Rwandan style in a plot somewhere in one of the cemeteries near Kigali. I didn't want people to be caught without a clue of what to do.

But as it turned out, I didn't die in Rwanda. In September of 2015 while I was on my regular annual visit to the states, I found myself pondering the question of my return more closely than I had yet done. True, it had been coming up more frequently lately. I'd had a health scare a couple of years earlier (it turned out to be a false alarm), and I was aging, and aware that I was not able to do as much as I had formerly done.

My visa as a missionary was up for renewal on November 9, and I wondered if the government would allow me to continue in the country after that date. Perhaps they would no longer consider that my presence was a benefit to the country. Other considerations were my son-in-law's illness (brain cancer) and my longing to be able to spend more time with my daughters before I got too old to enjoy them.

One of the goals of my leave time in the states was to clear out the things I had stored in my daughter Xan's barn. I had to make decisions about each thing—store elsewhere, toss, give away, or put in a yard sale. As two of my daughters and I went through this process, I began to have the feeling that I ought to continue to store some things, just in case I returned sooner rather than later. And so, I decided to rent a small storage unit, and we put some things there for the time being.

I believe God was gradually nudging me toward a decision to return soon—before the November 9 visa deadline, in fact. If they did refuse to renew my visa, that would leave me scrambling to wind up ten years of life in Rwanda in a very short time—maybe only twenty-four hours. It seemed better to be proactive, and plan the departure. I decided I would return from Rwanda to take up my life in America before November 9. That left just over five weeks to wrap things up. Once that decision was made, I had only three days left until my return to Rwanda.

God's welcome home

One concern I had about returning to the states was where to live. I knew that rentals were expensive, and I was envisioning either sharing an apartment with someone, renting a tiny studio, or maybe just a room in someone's house. In Rwanda, I had been renting a five-bedroom house with spacious grounds for about $750 per month. Friends were praying about this, and God had already prepared a home for me.

On the Monday before my flight left, I felt a strong inner nudge to go to Friendly Village, the mobile home park where I had owned a little home, and sold it—Unit 164—before going to Rwanda. I had loved that house—I had poured a lot of myself into it, refurbishing it, doing a little landscaping and enjoying gardening and cultivating potted plants on the deck I had built. It was a sunny and warm place, where I had welcomed friends, done spiritual direction, and enjoyed the companionship of my cat. As I have written earlier, it was a real sacrifice to give it up. Now, three days before returning to Rwanda for what was probably going to be the last time, here was this nudge, go to Friendly Village, and a thought came to me: perhaps there's a house there to buy. As I drove into the park—which is very pretty, with lots of trees, a salmon run creek and a historic covered bridge in a lovely green meadow—I said to the Lord, "If this is something you're doing, please give me clarity."

I went to the office and talked to the lady there. Did she know if any house was for sale in the park? She pointed me to a bulletin board, and there was a picture of Unit 164—my house—for sale! I was stunned; it seemed as though I ought to follow up on this.

After having the real estate agent come and show me the house—and finding it in very good condition, I told him I'd like to make an offer on it. I still had a little money from an inheritance I had received from my dad's estate. Within twenty-four hours, all the paperwork—including the necessary application to the park association—was done, and the house was mine! I arranged with my friend who had my power of attorney to follow up for me in the closing paperwork, which she did, and it closed as scheduled after I had returned to Rwanda. My friend would get the key and help direct friends to move my things from storage into the house before I returned. I felt embraced by God, affirmed in the decision I had made to return, and welcomed home in the best way imaginable.

How to end well in Rwanda

Having returned to Rwanda, I had about five weeks before I would leave for good. There were many people to see and say goodbye to. Friends came to the house—some more than once—bringing lovely, thoughtful gifts to remember them by. There was also the network: I had thought they would be ready to wrap things up, since Alexis and I were no longer around. I went to meet with the members, explaining that I was leaving, and asked them if they'd like to bring the network to an end. However, they had no such desire. They called two more meetings (on their own, without me) to decide exactly how they wanted to carry on, and then presented me with their decision: They would continue to meet on a quarterly basis, and carry out the activities they wanted to do as best they could, including visiting patients in hospitals and working on a sports outreach program. I was pleased with this, as it appeared the seed I had planted had taken root, and they were owning the vision. They prepared a wonderful luncheon farewell for me, and since the lunch was about two hours late, the intervening time was filled with warm salutes and remembrances of our time together. Each person needed to speak of how they felt—about me, and about the impact the network had on them. Rwandans never do any kind of ritual or celebration without speeches!

There was AEE, with which I had been affiliated for all those years. They had given me an office, though work space was at a premium, and supported me with prayer and encouragement in all the work I found to do, and I had made many good friends there. To send me on my way, they prepared a special luncheon, and of course, there were lots of speeches. When all the women were invited to come together to pray for me, many eyes were teary.

I made a plan to visit my old pastor Aaron, who had retired some years before, with his beautiful wife Jeanne, so I could tell them how much their ministry and fellowship had meant to me over the years. They seemed to appreciate that visit very much. (It also turned out to be an opportunity to give away my blender, which Jeanne needed and I wasn't planning to sell—she was so excited! She got up and threw her arms around me.) I was also visited at home by my new pastor, Julius, and a small delegation from that church where I had begun to be involved in the English service—preaching and advising when asked.

And of course, I had to deal with the house I had been renting, planning to sell or give away all my furniture and appliances. I was dreading that process, which would involve numbers of folks trooping in and out looking over the offerings and trying to make a good bargain. God had a better plan: a week had not elapsed since my return when my landlady came to tell me that she wanted to buy everything in the house herself, and she wanted me to leave everything just as it was—even the decorations I wasn't going to take with me (which was most of them). That was a huge help; it was all simply taken care of. What my landlady didn't want, I could find others who did—either to sell or give away—and that was part of the blessing God had prepared for me. For example, I had been given a beautiful handmade quilt for a thank you gift after participating in a friend's wedding. It was king size, and very heavy. I knew I could not take it back with me, limited as I was to four bags (two were free, and I paid extra for the others). It occurred to me that my friend Catherine, who with her Rwandan husband led the rich Ellel ministry (http://ellel.org/) which had blessed me, might like that quilt. She was indeed very happy about it, and so was I.

My little car needed to be sold, and again, I was expecting a complicated process—including having to pay an agent's fee. But God was way ahead of me. I was able to sell the car quickly—to the daughter of one of my oldest friends in Rwanda. It seemed just right for her to have it, and she was gracious to let me keep it until just before I left. I did love that car! It was a perky, bright red four-door Toyota Yaris, bought to replace my old RAV4. I'd had it raised up and equipped with larger tires so it could manage the bad roads without getting hung up on high bumps.

Since these logistics were being taken care of so smoothly, there was time and energy for ministry. In that last five weeks in Rwanda, God gave me opportunity to preach in three different churches—one of which was especially meaningful. From early in my network ministry, I had been very close to a young pastor called Dennis, who had a small organization called Hand to Heart, a member of the network. When the transition was made to Alexis as leader of the network, Dennis seemed to just disappear. He didn't come to meetings, nor did he answer phone calls or texts from me or Alexis. I was very worried about him, as well as hurt that he refused to respond to me, his "mom." I tried several times to reach him, but he either did not respond, or simply said he was fine.

Fruitful reconciliation

Now that I was leaving Rwanda for good, I felt I must try one more time to reach Dennis. This time when I texted him about meeting, he agreed—and we set a time. I still wondered if he would show up, as we had come that far before, and he had not appeared. But at the appointed time, there he was. We embraced warmly and sat on my veranda, as the day was fine and not too warm to sit outside. After the required ritual preamble, inquiring after our respective families and health, I invited Dennis to say what was on his heart regarding our long separation. He did. He had a great deal of resentment stored up against me and against the network members. I listened without comment as he poured out his hurt heart. When he was finished, I acknowledged his pain, and told him I was so sorry he had suffered in those ways. I also said I had no idea that we had hurt him so, and that I, for one, had no intention of hurting him, but I did apologize for the things I had done which he said had hurt him. I then told him how I too had been hurt by his long silence and refusal to be in fellowship with me. He could see that, and apologized. In the end, it seemed we had talked it all out, and were able to pray together and embrace each other in true loving reconciliation.

The special ministry was as a result of this reconciliation. Dennis invited me to come to his church to preach—and the only Sunday that would work was the next day. I gulped, then agreed, trusting that God would help me put together a sermon. By the end of the day, I had written what I knew was a powerful message on the importance of God's word in our lives. I was really excited to be able to share it, and I praised God so much for giving me this sermon so quickly and easily. Sunday dawned, and a problem soon emerged: I had diarrhea! As the early hours ticked away, I wondered how I was going to be able to go and preach. By what I considered to be the cut-off time, I simply got in the shower, prayed against the evil spirit of diarrhea (!) and got ready to go. I arrived about two hours before my time to preach, while the people were singing praise songs. I simply sat in my chair basking in the beautiful sound of their singing, as Dennis accompanied them skillfully on the keyboard. Praise was God's restorative, and by the time I was to preach, I was ready. Not only did I give the full sermon God had placed in my heart, but I came up with an illustration to further strengthen what I was saying. I spoke of the hidden Chinese church where Christians would keep bits and pieces of Scripture, guarding them closely, for the times they could meet together. I told these Rwandese how those Chinese believers valued God's word so much they were willing to die or be tortured if they were found out. I was confident I was preaching in the anointing of the Holy Spirit, blessing them and myself, and there is no greater joy than this.

As the days diminished and my time to leave drew close, I continued to see God's blessings, such as various fortuitous meetings and the last gathering in my house of the Tuesday morning ladies Bible study, which had been such a rich time for me over the years. Someone who worked outside Kigali even arranged to send by bus a special gift by relay through a friend, to give to my daughter Xan and her husband Humphrey. Then it was time to leave.

My landlord's family were going to occupy the house for a time until a new renter was found, and they had begun to move their things in while I was still there. I had a meltdown one evening, as they came into "my" house with beds and other furnishings, loudly chatting away to each other, oblivious of my feelings—and how could they know? I cried as I spoke to the sister who was managing this invasion, even while I knew I was being unreasonable. She was gracious, apologized, said she didn't know I would feel that way. Later, when it was time for me to leave, the whole family was there, kindly wishing me well.

My four bags were loaded into Gilbert's car. I wept as he drove me out the gate—I was leaving behind my beautiful garden brimming with zinnias, sunflowers, and canna lilies which my good gardener and general manager Sam had so carefully tended. I was leaving my home. A big part of my grief was because Sam wasn't there to say goodbye; he had not been able to get back from his village in time. He called me, and we said goodbye on the phone, but he was so dear and special to me, it was hard not to be able to give him a last hug.

As Gilbert drove, he said to me, "Mom, you have done so much for me over the years—everything I have and am is because of you." (He always says that, though I point out to him that he had a great part in his own success, and of course God made it possible.) "But," he continued, "I have one thing more to ask of you." I said, through my tears, "Gilbert, what is it?" He said, "Please don't forget me." Perhaps you can imagine how that didn't help me stop crying! Of course I wouldn't forget him—as I told him—he's my son!

Arrived at the airport. Bags unloaded by Gilbert. Many friends already waiting there to say goodbye—most of whom I had already had one-on-one goodbyes with. I just went around hugging everyone, and cameras were flashing. I needed to go—but just as I was almost in the line to check in, my dearest friend Jemrose came; I almost missed her in my hurry to get on with leaving, to get away from all the goodbyes. Some of her young people she's raising and training up to be good citizens of Rwanda (that's what her project is called—Young Citizens of Rwanda) came along, and I hugged them as well. Jemrose and I had made a pact to remain in contact and friendship, no matter what—and she promised to visit me in the states. It is not every person who gets to have such a close, dear friend and companion on the Way as we have been to each other.

Now it was time to go. Gilbert had paid an airport guy to help me with the bags all the way through the security and check in process, which was a great help—I wouldn't have been able to manage them by myself. My mind went on neutral, into travel mode. Checked in. Up the stairs. Into the coffee shop for a bite of supper. Into the waiting area. Somehow I was told to go get on the plane—didn't hear or register that my flight was called—and out onto the tarmac I went, rolling my little carry-on and sobbing. Looking across to that plane, it loomed like a monster ready to swallow me alive. Reached the bottom of the steps, feeling unable to manage even my small bag up those stairs. Crying. A man saying, "May I help you, madam?" and taking the bag up for me. I pulled myself up the stairs by the railing and into the plane. Crying still. Reaching my seat, I came to myself enough to stop weeping, in deference to my poor seat mate—it would be a long flight for him next to a hysterical old woman! And so I left Rwanda.

Meeting in Amsterdam

When my church's missions director learned of my decision to return for good from Rwanda, she hatched a crazy plan: She would fly from Seattle to Kigali and escort me home! The idea was to fly in the day before my flight, spend the night in Kigali, then help me finish up packing or whatever I needed, and fly with me—supplying tissues and an ear as needed on the way back. Who ever heard of such an extravagant idea? I didn't think I needed that, and it was expensive (though our church was graciously willing to pay for it). But I felt it was important to accept and be thankful for her offer, so I did.

As it turned out, she ran into a major glitch; she missed her flight to Kigali from Seattle, and there was simply no way for her to arrive in Rwanda in time to carry out her plan. But she is one determined lady; after hours of working with the airline agent, she found a flight that would get her to Amsterdam—my interim stop—before I arrived, and she could meet me there. Then she would carry out her plan to escort me home, at least on that last leg. And that's what she did. She got to Amsterdam hours before I arrived, spent the night in a hostel and returned to the airport early enough to be able to find me at the gate of the next leg.

She found me sitting at a coffee shop, overwhelmed and very alone. The sight of her filled me with joy! It turned out that her plan was what God had in mind—even if altered rather drastically from her original idea—because I could share with her some of the raw, new grief I was feeling, and she was ready with tissues and a warm, listening heart. The rest of the trip was a delight, because she was such a good traveling companion.

When we landed in Los Angeles, my daughter PJ met us with a bright bouquet, and my friend continued on to Seattle with three of my bags. PJ and I went to her home for a short rest and visit before we flew together to Seattle. Because of Humphrey's worsening condition with his brain cancer, we had planned to coordinate my return with a family gathering near Xan and Humphrey north of Bellingham, Washington, using a rental house as our base. That was an excellent time; although it was hard to see my son-in-law fading in his mental capacities, it was also beautifully moving to watch my daughter caring for him in always fresh and creative ways, showing her love for him.

Thus, my return to America was beautifully buffered by good family time, and I was set for the next phase: making my home once more in mobile home number 164.

14

Home Again?

MY RETURN TO MY church, my friends, and my own house was unexpectedly smooth. I was welcomed generously by my church; my missions pastor wanted to make sure they "got it right," making sure I knew how much I was loved and appreciated. A great team of fix-it folks blitzed my house, making lists of what needed to be done to make it livable and ship-shape, and then followed up to do everything on the list. As I entered into the fun process of figuring out how to furnish and decorate my house, relying heavily on thrift stores, I felt a flow of euphoria. I quickly found just the right pieces, and supplemented them with inexpensive furniture that needed to be assembled (and got great help with that). From November 9 through Christmas, I was on a roll. I kept wondering how I could be so happy, and what happened to reentry trauma, and the reverse culture shock everybody talked about? Although a lovely group of friends were poised to help me with any emotional struggles I might have, I never felt the need to call upon them. I was sailing!

I developed a theory, perhaps a revelation, about why I was doing so well: God had rescued me from Rwanda. By "rescue" I mean on a spiritual level. For some time—perhaps a couple of years—I had been sinking into a dangerous state of mind fueled by the Rwandan respect for age, and the tendency of people to want to do things for me. I was coming to believe I was *old*, and even feeble, and probably past having any real purpose in life. Although I was still doing a certain amount of teaching and preaching, I was nowhere near as busy as I had been in the early years. I seemed to be simply idling along. So, God got me out of there! He knew where my mind was heading, and wanted to snap me out of it. There's nothing like having to make a new home for yourself, in a brisk Pacific Northwest winter, to bring a person out of such a funk.

A shift in the wind

But then, my house was fully furnished, decorated in a way that pleased me, and there was nothing more to do in that area. My mood gradually began to shift, even as I filled my days with good things like exercise and diet and writing. I became slightly depressed, experiencing waves of great sadness and grief. I couldn't understand what was happening. And then there came a moment when I realized I was in a time warp: 2005 and 2015—the years of my departure and return—seemed seamlessly connected, and there was no reality to the ten years I had spent in Rwanda. I had no place to put them in my current experience, no way to incorporate them into who I was now. I decided to get some counseling help, which was good, and then made a decision to go for a debriefing retreat. My wonderful church had offered to send me for a debriefing, but until that time I hadn't felt I needed it. God is in charge of all things, including timing.

I can think of no better conclusion to this account of "a given life" than to tell of God's healing work at that debriefing week. Held in a Christian retreat center in Clarksville, Georgia, it was carried out by skilled and ex-perienced debriefers associated with Le Rucher Ministries, headquartered in France. This was the East Coast branch. For readers unfamiliar with the concept, debriefing is a means of helping people who have worked cross-culturally, or who have suffered any kind of traumatic experience, to dis-cover God's perspective and healing.

My experience was full of healing and freeing insights. I could not imagine how the week could have been any better. Through the easy pace of presentations of various tools to help us in our debriefing work, and daily meetings with our debriefers, the rhythms of healing began to flow from the first day. Gently and always with affirmations, my debriefer pointed out what she could see that God had done, and was now doing in my heart and life. I called her my "midwife"; she assisted at the birthing of new insights that had immediate healing effect.

There were three such insights from which I expect God to continue to flow healing into my life, relationships, and ministry. First, about the

Rwanda experience: I was given a new and freeing perspective, enabling me to see with joy that I had done very well in my ten years there. Not only did I figure out how to live and be in a radically different culture without the help of a mission board as many missionaries have, but I also created and sustained ministries that tested and stretched me. In the process, God built new gifts into me that I can continue to use in the states. I could happily and with praise set Rwanda in its place in my heart and mind.

Second, God led me back to the most grievous sin in my life. I have written about this above. I had continued to feel anguish about it, and God showed me three things: First, by persisting in that grief over my sin, I was dishonoring my Lord who died to save me from all sin. Second, in the process I was holding onto a false belief that I should be punished for my sin. I had lived all those years with an inner demand for justice against the perpetrator—who was me. I could now see that within me were two entities bound together as with chains: myself, the perpetrator, and myself, the judge who would never let the perpetrator off the hook. Once I saw this truth, the lie slunk away, and the bonds were broken.

Third, and in some ways most wonderful, I discovered that I had been living with a shame-based self-awareness, stemming from birth. When I reviewed those circumstances, my mother dying as a result of having me, I saw how my father's blame had landed squarely on me. I realized that I could stand with Jesus against the lie Satan placed in my heart while still a baby: I am shameful! I don't deserve to exist. Now the lie was unmasked, and the truth of God's purpose in creating me was clear to me. I am a new creation in Christ, renouncing shame once and for all.

I am grateful to and for all the Le Rucher staff for their gracious and humble leadership. I trust God to always be creating something new for me. As long as I have breath, my desire is to stay in his service. As the world careens into darker and darker ways, I know that a big part of my work now is to let my heart break and let God's love flow into the cracks, outward in ministry, upward in prayer.

15

Gleanings

WHAT FOLLOWS IS A selection of writings from my journals over the years in Rwanda, special moments I felt God was revealing himself and his ways to me. I share them in the hope that they might perhaps encourage others as well.

Perspective on creativity

The purpose and use of God's perfect and voluminous creation is, maybe, to provide the materials for artists, poets, and songwriters to discover what is hidden there. They tease it out, and draw it into forms to delight, amaze, and at times shock and awe the rest of us. They show us what lies within, beyond, under the otherwise untold immensities and minutiae of all that comes from the mouth of God. Glory be to God for his singers and poets, his artisans and artists, his novelists and theologians, his composers and scientists and mathematicians—all glory to him—for the potential of all of these makers and discoverers to embellish and make dear and lovely the deep things God has hidden for them to find.

And shame to us, who twist and sully the discoveries and hidden wonders for our own greedy and grievous ends—to our end. The dark makers—poets, singers, artists—whose only purpose is to obfuscate truth, wonder, and delight, whose bent minds and hearts crave destruction, pain, excess of ecstasy, oblivion—woe to them, and to us if we open our eyes and ears and minds to them, even a little. And how can we avoid it? They are everywhere—in the glimpses of an unknown movie to see if we might like it, in a gift shop that has beautiful things, but also deposits of this slime scattered about to trap the unwary. Jesus prayed that God would protect his disciples from the Evil One as they remained in the world. How we ought so to pray for ourselves and one another!

Turn the eyes, the heart, the mind and ears to those beauties and pure melodies given us by the Creator through his cocreator children—and rejoice that such images and songs can still be seen and heard. And join them. Use the eyes God has given you to see into things and bring out for others the truths and beauties you find. You belong with them.

Hunger and thirst for God

Ps 119:20, Gimel: "My soul is consumed with longing for your ordinances at all times." Longing for, while yet always loving and keeping God's statutes. What would my life be like if I had this momentary longing? The more one clings to God's ways, the more one wants them to be manifested and revealed. Verse 20 reminds me of Jesus' words: "Blessed are those who hunger and thirst after righteousness, for they will be filled" (Matt 5:6). The hungering and thirsting continues—as here, the longing—even while it is satisfied by God, by his word. This hunger is not like physical hunger. Satiety in God never produces the kind of fullness that pushes away from him as we push away from the table. On the other hand, after eating, we always get hungry again and come back to the table. That pictures this spiritual longing and satisfaction; we are filled, satisfied—for a time—and then again hungry. The difference is that for spiritual food we can be hungry *and* satisfied simultaneously, and never stuffed as after a great feast. Lord, allow me to be "consumed" (strange word: as I eat your word, I am "eaten" by desire for more) by longing for your word.

Teach me your way

"Teach me O Lord the way of your statutes, and I will observe it to the end" (Ps 119:33). The psalmist writes from humility—*teach* me! I don't know everything, but I love your word, and know you are the best one to teach it. I need to be taught. The *way* of your statutes: what pathway your word lays out, what boundaries, what valleys and mountains to traverse, what path through dark and treacherous places where self-pity, impatience, and bitterness are like sinking sands for my feet unless they know the way of your statutes. If you teach me—as you taught the crowds sitting on the grass—and I delight as they did in your gracious, wise, startling, homely teaching—I will observe, obey, follow the way *until the end*—the end of the way, the destination which is you, Lord, yourself and the Father, the end of my life on earth. Teach me your way, from your word, and help me to stay on it to the end.

Halo

I have glimpsed what the halo in paintings might be depicting: the glow of a person receiving your gifts, Lord, of joy and love and wisdom and peace, poured out to us, and us returning praise to you, never-ending, a golden circle. I saw, just in a moment this morning, how I need to receive from you, Lord. I need all that you give. Your gifts are life-sustaining, not just extra blessings, like icing on a cake. I can't imagine life without your gifts—*yourself* poured into my heart as love—you are love. This frustration about not having electricity has drawn my attention to this truth: that it is *you* that I need, and all else will be well. Let me drink deeply, feed fully, on you, in you, of you. Otherwise I'm like a "wineskin in smoke."

Useless to complain

Oh these bites! I continue to itch and lose sleep—and also am taking good steps, making progress, toward patience. God is producing this in me. I see what a temptation complaining is, and how useless, and how difficult to resist—almost like resisting the urge to scratch the bites! I can complain, and it seems to relieve the pressure for a moment, but then the burden seems even heavier. So, I *refuse* to complain; I *choose* to rejoice. It works, praise God! Only, I do feel free to pour out my complaint to him, with praise, throwing myself on his strength, reassurance, comfort, and protection.

Tears in prayer

When I pray for my friend, great racking sobs come out. It is surely the Holy Spirit—as soon as I stop praying, the tears end, and I am not left with any burden or fatigue. It is a privilege God is giving me, and sustaining me in my weakness. "May those who sow in tears reap with shouts of joy (Ps 126:5). Because of this new experience of weeping in prayer for others, I see a new meaning in this verse, and promise for my prayers. Certainly when they are answered I will have great joy—even greater than the tears of anguish, longing, and warfare in prayer.

I need to humble myself, and be on guard against exalting experience in prayer over the *Lord* of prayer. . . . Gracious God, you have helped me understand the tears—of course! They come from the love you have given me for those I pray for. How obvious, now!

Chicken or eagle?

Devotion needs renewing—I saw that I am more like a chicken than an eagle in the Spirit. Cried out to Jesus, who accepted me and blessed me with tears, my tears, his love, and my love in him. I desire that all the things I am doing find their life and purpose in Jesus. All is only busyness unless endowed and endued with the Spirit and love of Jesus. I seek renewal in him. I have no time these days for various sweet interruptions, as people used to come and find me available. Now I'm in a meeting all the time, or planning one. Lord Jesus, please show me your way, so that all things will be done in your strength and will and for your glory.

Harmful luxury

Aware of grieving over sins; how gracious God is to make me know I have done wrong, so as to seek his cleansing and renewal, and help in making what amends I can. If it weren't for him, I would not know or care that I behaved badly and much more damage would follow, as though I un- wittingly tracked mud into the house and walked around everywhere. Sin usurps love. When I choose a sinful way—attitude, manner of speaking, etc.—love has no place, falls away, is helpless on the sidelines. When I re- gard a person through the eyes of "righteous" indignation, love is blinded. I see only an offender before me. What harm can occur in that blinded state! The relationship I treasure is threatened by even one moment of irritation, impatience, anger. As one who has received mercy, let me extend all mercy, and forego the harmful luxury of irritation.

Only trust God

Long time praying against the wall in tears, and on my knees—God helped me to pray in Kinyarwanda. Realized the need for and prayed for more love—from him to me, to cover the multitude of my sins. And he does love me. Thanks and praise are due to him. If I can only stay in his love, that would be good. I talked to him about all the work I am doing, wondering if it is I who has taken all, or much, of it on, out of some self-drive to be super-woman—it is truly too much for me! And I feel that God told me simply to trust him—even if it is so that I have taken on more than he would have given me. Trust him in it—*trust* him, who loves me and understands me, and knows what he wants to bring forth in and through me. If I trust and wait upon him, no matter what happens, he will be glorified.

Two masters

We four are working at two desks, surrounded by boxes and packets
we are supposed to be giving to people in need.
Entering data from uncertain sources, behind deadline,
struggling with formats and unfamiliar software.
A spirit of irritation, another of self-pity leer at me
from the dust that makes me sneeze. No one is happy.
All agree the task is difficult, but we will do it.
We can only manage by keeping kindness for each other.
This is a time when there is simply no space for pouting.

I pout, nevertheless. I wasn't expecting this kind of work.
I wasn't supposed to have to perch my laptop on a box
and cram my knees against its sides. I wasn't supposed to . . .
according to whom? Who is in charge of my life?
Am I my only master? I have the choice to work at this,
to help, when so much work needs doing, or to slip away,
claim age, or that it's not in line with my calling.
If I choose to stay and work, my Master asks for patience.
And cheerfulness. My choice.
I love the way he leads me! No choice.

God will rise up

"Because of the oppression of the weak and the groaning of the needy, I will now arise," says the Lord. "I will protect them from those who malign them" (Ps 12:5). God's promise, to be fulfilled through prayer, faith, yielding to him as his instruments. I am his partial answer if I am willing. I am willing, Lord; make me much more willing—not by might, nor by power, but by your Spirit, all is possible. God will now rise up, he says. Those whose responsibility it is to protect and help the poor are instead wasting their time in lying to each other about their own autonomy: "our lips are our own—who is our master?" Meanwhile, and because these people have neglected them, the needy groan. But God says he will now rise up "and place them in the safety for which they long." He will not do this apart from us whom he has appointed as his ambassadors, servants, instruments—his agents by the Spirit of Christ within us.

Open the gates!

"Lift up your heads, O gates, and be lifted up, O ancient doors, that the King of glory may come in" (Ps 24:7). Lift up what is closed, protecting from of old, but no longer needed for protection. Let the King of glory, the Lord of Hosts, come in. What are these gates? *Amarembo.* Tradition, ritual, habits of self-protection, self-indulgence. Secrecy and jealousy. Fear of being taken advantage of. Locked down mentality—hopelessness, fatalism. Lift up these gates, these ancient doors! Let the King come in. The King of glory is coming. Let him in. Open the gates.

More grace

Praise to God, the Lord. He loves and sustains and refreshes, though my sins are confronting me daily, yet God gives more grace. Truly, the more I sin—inadvertently, not maliciously—the more God seems to give grace, so that I am humbled, repentant, bowed down before him who knows me so well yet continues to love, rebuke, correct, and restore me.

Hagar's consolation

"Then God opened her eyes and she saw a well of water" (Gen 21:19). Hagar had been completely despairing of life for herself and Ishmael; she had been sent away from Abraham to wander in the desert, and there was no water left. Then God opened her eyes and she saw a well of water. It seems to say that water was already there, but Hagar hadn't been able to see it until God opened her eyes. God, would you open my eyes to see what refreshment is there for me? I am in need of it. My life seems to be coming to an end with no purpose or strength. *Yet*, I know you are with me and will still guide me and show me what I am at the moment unable to see. If you did this for the slave woman, how much more will you do something similar for me, your child? In my blankness, emptiness, I wait for you, Lord.

No condemnation

Reading in Matt 25. Why do I hear only the condemnation in these passages? The kingdom of God requires that we watch for the Lord's return, that we be good stewards of his things entrusted to us, and that we carry out his compassionate ministry. If we do not, we will be cast out, not welcomed. I fear not measuring up to all these requirements. I don't hear grace and acceptance in the Beloved, only condemnation. What is my problem? This cuts very deep, touches a long-held fear, perhaps, of rejection because of not measuring up.

I ask you, Lord, to expose and deal with this fear, or further enlighten me. Surely you, King of kings, have a right to expect and require certain behaviors and actions from your subjects. And it is part of your word—your intention—that we should share your inheritance and happiness. *But*, only a few will end up doing so—many invited, few chosen. I cling to the word which assures me of salvation through faith in the blood of Christ, as I also do what I can to measure up—but *knowing* I never will. Alas! But Jesus, you have made me yours. Why should I fear? Nothing can separate me from your love. You stand in heaven as my advocate, you who have the right to condemn me.

Keeping my eyes on Jesus

Habits can be broken. Lord, I need your help with this. Would you give me something to remind me to be mindful of you as I go along in my day? An image, a word? I'm to "lay aside every weight," it says in Heb 12:1, everything that hinders; what things, Lord? Anything that makes me stumble or struggle unnecessarily on the way, anything that entangles or impedes my walk. Ways of reacting, mind-set, how I treat others—things I have control over; the illusion of control, such that I take my eyes off Jesus, author and perfecter of my faith.

Lord, these are generalities; can you, would you, reveal specifics? Capture my gaze, Lord. Laziness in me? Too much work, to keep my eyes on you? I think of lovers—one thing they do is gaze into each other's eyes. They don't tire of doing so. They have an intimacy which doesn't intimidate them, but draws them closer and closer, as though they could become one by simply locking eyes. Jesus, you are the Lover of my soul, and you have captured my heart. Help me, Lord my Love, to let myself look into your eyes.

Does "keeping your eyes on Jesus" mean *this?* Locking into his gaze? Have I ever done so? No, I don't think so. It seems to frighten me. Perhaps I still cannot believe in such a love. The only way is through faith.

The fellowship of suffering

Reminded of Phil 3:10: "That I may know him and the power of his resurrection, and may share his sufferings, becoming like him in his death." I think this "fellowship in his sufferings" is what Shane Claiborne is talking about as he describes what ought to be our "ordinary radicalism" as Christians.[1] I shrink from suffering, and miss out on the fellowship that comes from sharing in Christ's sufferings—in the lives of all the poor and outcast. Much of my life is a sham. Yes, I've sold up and gone to Rwanda—while still protecting my privacy and comfort. I engage with the poor and outcast somewhat, on my careful terms. I don't allow myself to get too hot, tired, or dirty. If I'm to know Christ, and the power of his resurrection, I must accept and even welcome the sharing of his sufferings which, if I understand this, provides a fellowship—with Jesus, and others—that nothing else can.

---

1. Claiborne, *Irresistible Revolution.*

Testing

God is testing us. What does this mean? At one extreme, there is Abraham's test when God told him to sacrifice Isaac, the son of the promise. On a microscopic level, comparatively, testing is also an issue in many areas of daily life: driving tests in order to get a permit; my testing Adalbert, who is studying English, so I could see what he had learned. In these cases, the test proves a level of achievement. Testing occurs all through our lives. We are always being moved along from one level to another, receiving certificates, diplomas, permits, etc., to mark successful completion.

But God tests his people too. I would think he wouldn't need to—he knows everything. But *does* he know how we will measure up? He operates with us in time, yet from a perspective of eternity, of omniscience. Moses was instructing the Israelites to obey God, so as to receive the blessing— and yet he *knew* they would fail and disobey God, and be expelled from the land (just as Adam and Eve had failed and were expelled). Even so with us; God instructs us to obey and follow him, knowing we will fail much of the time. But not *all* of the time. Abraham didn't fail that test.

In our trials, God is testing us to know whether we will trust him. Without the tests, we will never be sure of the genuineness of our faith. A soldier worried about being a coward on the battlefield will never know if he is brave unless he is plunged into battle. I can see that it benefits *us* to find out if we can pass God's tests, but am still puzzled about God's angle. Is there something about the human character, made in God's image, that is inscrutable even to God, until it reveals itself through testing? In any case, to be sure of passing the tests in life, and the ultimate test, as Abraham and Jesus faced, I must practice obedience and faith and loving acceptance all along the way—in every small thing—so as to build up these muscles and be able to stand "in the evil day."

How wonderful God is! He prepares us well for all the hard tests because he wants us to pass. He never allows any area of our formation to lapse, but continually watches over all aspects of our lives in the Spirit. If there is a weakness or lack in us, he knows how to make us feel our need of him, so as to cry out to him for the help he is ready to give. This is a good reason to rejoice in times of trial.

Thanksgiving

I come to the awareness or perhaps decision that my life be a thanksgiving to God, *incarnated thanks,* for all he has done and is doing in me to save and redeem and renew me. In all things give thanks, Paul says. There is no way I can adequately thank God for all he is and does; only by my life, my activities, ministry, conversations, gifts—all rendered in thanksgiving, as physical outworking of a thankful heart.

Fear not

How good it will be to have my glorified, resurrection body! What joy, to move freely, in all dimensions, and surely, to fly! Otherwise why dream of flying? The "law" of gravity will somehow be overcome, or things will simply know their true position relative to everything else, though those positions may be fluid, not fixed. Lord, selfishly, I'd not mind coming there any time, but that is *truly* selfish, or maybe, just in sync with all creation, groaning to be set free from bondage to decay.

The Lord has shown me how much my peace and security depend on a sound body. I must learn to relinquish this dependency and fling myself wholly on the Lord who is my life, now and always. The journey ahead into old age and death is inevitable—there's no turning back, no choice but to go forward—either in increasing weakness due to fear, or in increasing faith due to the abiding presence of the Lord who loves me. That *is* a choice—as in everything that comes to us, to trust and rest in the loving care of my Father in heaven, or to tremble and cringe and shrink back, shrivel up in fear. My default surely is fear. But with the Lord's persistent help I can reset, or override that default. So often God's angel appears to one or another and says, "Fear not," and, "I am with you."

Suffering is a necessary part of life, and it accomplishes something nothing else can. Jesus came to suffer on our behalf and at our hands. Suffering is something God does—for us, and with us, and because of us. How can I ask why God waits to rescue or help people who are suffering, when God himself suffers with them and for them? Suffering brings people together as nothing else can. It shows people they need each other, and God. Suffering is a crucible—precious yield comes out.

Loving God's commands

In prayer, reviewing and praising God for his grace in dying for me, for all the world, flowing tears as usual of joy and gratitude—how great a salvation! And the grace that secures it to me, and me in it, to the end. As I prayed, "thy will be done," I became aware of a new-to-me thought: I love the Lord's commands! How precious they are to me. He commands me in tender love, compelling instant and glad obedience. Such joy in this swift obedience. And when he does not specifically command me, he leads me—of that I am confident.

Invitation

Good morning, Lord. I am here, and I believe you are here with me. I am ready to read your word, and want to listen for your still, small voice as I read. You know how attentive I can be, and how distracted. Be gracious, Lord Jesus, my Redeemer, to call my spirit to attention so that I will not miss what you have for me now. What I will read I have read many times before over the years. In your mercy, Lord, my Lord, let me hear with new awareness, refreshed understanding. Let that old veil of pride, which like a cataract can dim my vision, be excised, pulled away, lifted. Without your Holy Spirit, Lord, I can understand nothing, and therefore can do nothing that pleases you. I acknowledge you, God, as sovereign and all-powerful and ageless, and also present and personal to me, your beloved child. How can this be? I can't grasp it except by faith, which is also your gift to me. Sovereign Lord, Beloved Companion, draw me up and out of myself through the reading and understanding of your word, and call me to obedience which is true love of you.

Control

One main bar in me to being fully fruitful is control. I have settled into the notion that I can, or need to, control the level of my work, service to God and his people, to hold back, ride the brakes, avoid going so fast with God that I lose my illusion of control. It is as always a failure in faith. I simply don't trust God to manage my life such that I can accept the level of activity required. I am the clay; he is the potter. I live in dangerous forgetfulness of that reality. I don't *have* control. All I have is rebellion, resistance to God's will. I confess that, it is sin, and release it. God, who knows me, who knows the number of the days of my life, who knows the plans he has for me, not for evil, but to give me a future and a hope—this God is sovereign, and he *is* in control. All resistance is destructive, hurtful, useless, and delays the accomplishment of God's will in me—which is unique to me. Lord, this issue in one guise or another continues to raise its ugly head. I must thank you for each reminder, and each call to release my puny idea of control, repent and move toward you for more fruit for the glory which is yours.

Sin's wretchedness

How long, O Lord? The people are so overwhelmed by Satan's numerous tactics to deceive, steal, and kill, and have become wicked, cruel, heartless, lacking in compassion, suspicious, ready to believe any lie without investigation—even those who call themselves Christians. I am miserable as I think of how wretched people are because of sin. May it be soon, Lord, that you will come! Long ago, Jeremiah wept for the unbelief and unfaithfulness of your people, and now, Lord, it goes on, even after Jesus came to relieve and rescue us all from sin. Come, Lord Jesus! And may your people rise up, *now*, and fight for the way of truth, love, true peace, reconciliation, and unity of the body of Christ. We can't just be passive, waiting for you to return—we are your body, with your clear instructions, to love and serve and sacrifice in this world, until you come. May we be found faithful in this. May I be found faithful, Adonai.

Prayer instruction

As I prayed, the Lord instructed me to pray thus: *Rule me, and teach me to rule*—even here on this earth, so I can have an idea of ruling with you in the New Earth/Heaven. And, *Let me see you, God, with my eyes of faith*, so that I will recognize you when I see you with the eyes of the resurrected body.

Our God speaks

"Man does not live by bread alone, but man lives by every word that comes from the mouth of the Lord" (Deut 8:3b). We do need bread, but there is a life beyond the life that can be sustained by bread. We are sustained as eternal beings, children of God, by "every word" God speaks. We have a speaking God. Words, one by one, come from his mouth. As opposed to idols, which have mouths carved or painted by men but cannot speak, our God speaks, *so that* we may live. He also provides our daily bread, knowing our physical need. But our real life is nourished upon his every word. Jesus relied upon the sustenance of God's word in the desert and resisted Satan's temptation to prove himself God's Son by turning stones into bread. Because he *was* the Son of God, he knew where his life came from, and relied upon that speaking source. How do I rely upon God's every word for nourishment of my true life? Read, ponder, take it in with understanding, through prayer—and obey. Jesus is the word made flesh, who imparts life to me as I trust in him.

Hid with Christ in God

In 2 Chr 22, it says Jehoshabeath hides her one-year-old nephew Joash so as to protect him from wicked Athaliah. This reminded me of the verse in Col 3:3 where it says, "For you have died, and your life is hidden with Christ in God." We have died—to ourselves, the world, our former life—yet we live; as Paul says in Gal 2:20, "It is no longer I who live, but Christ who lives in me." The only life I have now is Christ's. I *keep* coming back to this: "You are not your own, for you were bought with a price" (1 Cor 16:19–20). [A] meditation on humility.

I see more now about meditation on the word. It is like holding a beautiful stone with polished planes, and some left natural with perhaps some inner gleams, taking note of what is there. But in God's word, there are always unmined depths, unglimpsed insights, if one is willing to keep turning it around—maybe seeming to see the same things over and over. As I am willing to submit to looking, it may be that I will see something new—or perhaps not. It takes humility to truly meditate, willingness to leave the position of knowing and enter the low door of givenness. What is there, is for me now—not to master, as with academics, but to receive and welcome and admire.

Analogy

To enter into what God is doing—seeing where and how he is working and being ready to participate—is like being a surgeon's nurse: watching closely where the surgeon is working, anticipating his or her needs, ready instantly to slap the right instrument into the surgeon's hands. Like a surgeon it is a life-enhancing, even life-saving work God is doing.

Yoked with Christ for the whole journey

To realize I am yoked with Jesus means to walk at his pace. To know that I am a coworker with him (2 Cor 6:1) means he has not only gone ahead to prepare the territory, already knows the language, knows each person I'll be meeting, but is also alongside me—yoked to *me*, as I am to him. It is his humility that takes my pace and trains it to his.

A beggar and a daughter's prayer

I came to a new understanding about prayer, received as I prayed: to pray as a beggar—one who desperately needs what he asks for, in solidarity and identification with those who have such deep needs as for shelter, protection, food, water, health, and knowledge of Christ's love—but praying as a daughter of the King, who knows the Father's heart and fully expects him to release good things for those I pray for. We are *called* to pray by Jesus. God help me to *get* it, that prayer is essential—not that I understand why, but that it is the way God works in this world.

Three terrains

God is so gracious to meet his wayward child! He shows me new things about his leading—a glimpse of three terrains that he brings me safely through: a jungle, a great tangle and confusion and cacophony, many paths made by animals, but no way to know the right path without him; a desert, where the wind sweeps away pathways and footprints; a swamp, where no path is, but he shows me safe footholds. "All other ground is sinking sand." He has given me "beauty for ashes, joy instead of mourning, praise instead of despair" (Isa 61:3).

Bibliography

Bangley, Bernard, ed. *Nearer to the Heart of God: Daily Readings with the Christian Mystics.* Brewster, MA: Paraclete, 2005.

Berry, Wendell. *This Day: Collected and New Sabbath Poems.* Berkeley: Counterpoint, 2013.

Claiborne, Shane. *The Irresistible Revolution: Living as an Ordinary Radical.* Grand Rapids: Zondervan, 2006.

Haslam, David F., ed. "Robert Murray M'Cheyne's Bible Reading Calendar." The Robert Murray M'Cheyne Resource, January 2000. http://www.mcheyne.info/calendar.pdf.

Jones, David Hugh, ed. *The Hymnbook.* Richmond, VA: Presbyterian Church in the United States, 1955.

May, Gerald G. *The Dark Night of the Soul: A Psychiatrist Explores the Connection Between Darkness and Spiritual Growth.* San Francisco: HarperSanFrancisco, 2004.